Microprocessor 3

Series Editor
Jean-Charles Pomerol

Microprocessor 3

Core Concepts – Hardware Aspects

Philippe Darche

WILEY

First published 2020 in Great Britain and the United States by ISTE Ltd and John Wiley & Sons, Inc.

ISTE Ltd
27-37 St George's Road
London SW19 4EU
UK

www.iste.co.uk

John Wiley & Sons, Inc.
111 River Street
Hoboken, NJ 07030
USA

www.wiley.com

Library of Congress Control Number: 2020942119

British Library Cataloguing-in-Publication Data
A CIP record for this book is available from the British Library
ISBN 978-1-78630-565-7

Contents

Quotation

Every advantage has its disadvantages and vice versa.

Shadokian philosophy[1]

---

1 The Shadoks are the main characters from an experimental cartoon produced by the Research Office of the Office de Radiodiffusion-Télévision Française (ORTF). The two-minute-long episodes of this daily cult series were broadcast on ORTF's first channel (the only one at the time!) beginning in 1968. The birds were drawn simply and quickly using an experimental device called an *animograph*.

The Shadoks are ridiculous, stupid and mean. Their intellectual capacities are completely unusual. For example, they are known for bouncing up and down, but it is not clear why! Their vocabulary consists of four words: GA, BU, ZO and MEU, which are also the four digits in their number system (base 4) and the musical notes in their four-tone scale. Their philosophy is comprised of famous mottos such as the one cited in this book.

Preface

Computer systems (hardware and software) are becoming increasingly complex, embedded and transparent. It therefore is becoming difficult to delve into basic concepts in order to fully understand how they work. In order to accomplish this, one approach is to take an interest in the history of the domain. A second way is to soak up technology by reading datasheets for electronic components and patents. Last but not least is reading research articles. I have tried to follow all three paths throughout the writing of this series of books, with the aim of explaining the hardware and software operations of the microprocessor, the modern and integrated form of the central unit.

About the book

This five-volume series deals with the general operating principles of the microprocessor. It focuses in particular on the first two generations of this programmable component, that is, those that handle integers in 4- and 8-bit formats. In adopting a historical angle of study, this deliberate decision allows us to return to its basic operation without the conceptual overload of current models. The more advanced concepts, such as the mechanisms of virtual memories and cache memory or the different forms of parallelism, will be detailed in a future book with the presentation of subsequent generations, that is, 16-, 32- and 64-bit systems.

The first volume addresses the field's introductory concepts. As in music theory, we cannot understand the advent of the microprocessor without talking about the history of computers and technologies, which is presented in the first chapter. The second chapter deals with storage, the second function of the computer present in the microprocessor. The concepts of computational models and computer architecture will be the subject of the final chapter.

The second volume is devoted to aspects of communication in digital systems from the point of view of buses. Their main characteristics are presented, as well as their communication, access arbitration, and transaction protocols, their interfaces and their electrical characteristics. A classification is proposed and the main buses are described.

The third volume deals with the hardware aspects of the microprocessor. It first details the component's external interface and then its internal organization. It then presents the various commercial generations and certain specific families such as the Digital Signal Processor (DSP) and the microcontroller. The volume ends with a presentation of the datasheet.

The fourth volume deals with the software aspects of this component. The main characteristics of the Instruction Set Architecture (ISA) of a generic component are detailed. We then study the two ways to alter the execution flow with both classic and interrupt function call mechanisms.

The final volume presents the hardware and software aspects of the development chain for a digital system as well as the architectures of the first microcomputers in the historical perspective.

Multi-level organization

This book gradually transitions from conceptual to physical implementation. Pedagogy was my main concern, without neglecting formal aspects. Reading can take place on several levels. Each reader will be presented with introductory information before being asked to understand more difficult topics. Knowledge, with a few exceptions, has been presented linearly and as comprehensively as possible. Concrete examples drawn from former and current technologies illustrate the theoretical concepts.

When necessary, exercises complete the learning process by examining certain mechanisms in more depth. Each volume ends with bibliographic references including research articles, works and patents at the origin of the concepts and more recent ones reflecting the state of the art. These references allow the reader to find additional and more theoretical information. There is also a list of acronyms used and an index covering the entire work.

This series of books on computer architecture is the fruit of over 30 years of travels in the electronic, microelectronic and computer worlds. I hope that it will provide you with sufficient knowledge, both practical and theoretical, to then specialize in one of these fields. I wish you a pleasant stroll through these different worlds.

IMPORTANT NOTES. — As this book presents an introduction to the field of microprocessors, references to components from all periods are cited, as well as references to computers from generations before this component appeared.

Original company names have been used, although some have merged. This will allow readers to find specification sheets and original documentation for the mentioned integrated circuits on the Internet and to study them in relation to this work.

The concepts presented are based on the concepts studied in selected earlier works (Darche 2000, 2002, 2003, 2004, 2012), which I recommend reading beforehand.

Philippe DARCHE
July 2020

Introduction

The microprocessor is almost 50 years old. Since its arrival, its performance has grown steadily thanks to advances in the integration of microelectronics. This component has transformed the computer industry and is behind the microcomputer. Today, it is at the heart of digital systems, embedded or not, and supercomputers.

The purpose of this volume is to present the basic principles of its operation from the hardware angle with many industrial examples. For the latter, if a choice has to be made among the commercial processors, we will choose in a privileged way the 8- and 16-bit categories because they have all the characteristics desired for an educational approach. Their characteristics will be compared with reference computer architectures such as the VAX (Virtual Addressed eXtended) minicomputer. We start with a definition and a brief history. Then, we approach its external interface. Then, we are interested in its internal functioning. Its programming will be discussed in the next volume.

NOTE.– The examples given refer to microprocessors and current and past computer processors.

1

Basic and Historical Definitions

This chapter, introduction to the field, presents after the basic definitions, a history. In this context, the key characteristics of the microprocessors representative of these five decades are given.

1.1. Basic definitions

A microprocessor or MPU (MicroProcessor[1] Unit) is the integrated version of the central processing unit[2] (CPU) of computers from the 1960s, the prefix "micro" referring to miniaturization[3]. The central unit was made up of several electronic cards at the time where many integrated circuits in DIP (Dual-In-Line Package; *cf.* § 3.3 of Darche (2004)) were installed. These cards communicated with each other using a backplane bus (*cf.* § V2-4.2.7). The architecture of the microprocessor therefore inherits that of the central processing units of previous computers, themselves resulting from the von Neumann model (*cf.* § V1-3.2.2) for almost all. Of course, all of the current features, such as virtual memory (VM) or cache (this will be covered in a future book), were only gradually integrated due to the integration limitations of the technologies of the time.

---

1 The term "microprocessor" was used for the first time by the company Viatron Computer Systems Corporation in 1968 to name its terminal System 21 2140/2150 (Computers and Automation 1968; Bassett 2002) of which the CPU consisted only of discrete logic components of type MSI/LSI.

2 In the sense of Chapter 3 of Volume 1, that is, without integrated primary memory (for now!).

3 It should not be associated with that of microprogramming (this will be covered in a future book by the author on microprocessors) because the control of a microprocessor is not necessarily microprogrammed. It can be wired.

This component is in the form of a single Integrated Circuit (IC) in monolithic version, originally belonging to the LSI category (Large-Scale Integration; *cf.* § V1-1.2) and developed in PMOS technology (positive (channel) metal-oxide semiconductor; *cf.* § 2.1.3 of Darche (2004)). Today, the microprocessor, essentially CMOS technology (Complementary MOS; *cf.* § 2.4 of Darche (2004)), offers parallel hardware execution. Exceptions included where the microprocessor was a set of integrated circuits, an example being the iAPX 432 (Witten and Cleary 1983) of the company Intel made up of three integrated circuits but that remained marginal.

From a logical point of view, a microprocessor is a sequential system (*cf.* Chapter 3 of Darche (2002)) programmable, synchronous[4] most of the time, which executes a program, that is, an ordered sequence of instructions, stored in a so-called central, main or primary memory, volatile or not. We can see it as a complex form of state machine (FSM for Finite-State Machine; *cf.* § 3.7.3 of Darche (2002)).

Its basic instructions make it possible to carry out the logical and arithmetic processing of information and to carry out a transfer of control. To do this, it has three functions, calculation, storage and transfer of information.

When it integrates memory and Input/Output (I/O) controllers, it becomes a microcontroller or MCU (MicroController or MicroComputer Unit; *cf.* § 5.3) including the TMS 1000 from the company Texas Instruments (TI – 1974) was the first representative. The microprocessor can be general purpose (multipurpose or general-purpose MPU, GPP for General-Purpose Processor) or specialized in an application domain (ASP for Application-Specific Processor or ASIP for Application-Specific Instruction set Processor). The Digital Signal Processor (*cf.* 5.2) is a microprocessor specializing in digital signal processing, which is found, for example, in home video amplifiers. A subcategory of ASP is the bespoke processor (Moore 2017), a proposal by Cherupalli (2017) where the custom architecture is automatically generated to meet the needs of applications with high energy constraints such as the Internet of Things (IoT). The fields of use of the microprocessor are obviously IT, micro or classic, but industrial embedded systems are the real market. Since 2000, the trend has always been towards more integration. This has led to the emergence of systems-on-chip (SoCs, *cf.* § V1-1.2 and § V2-4.2.9), which involves the integration of an entire digital system, that is, multiple processors, memory and I/O controllers, into a single chip.

By extension, a processor is a reduction of a microprocessor in the sense that it contains at least one control unit, a calculation unit and registers. Today we also talk of core. The latter term appeared with the integration on the same chip of several cores in

---

4 The asynchronous version is envisaged for reasons of power consumption and signal propagation time, but it remains marginal industrially.

2001 (multicore approach) with, today (2018), a dozen cores integrated on industrial chips. This trend was a response to the powerwall (*cf.* § V1-1.5), which materializes the physical limit.

1.2. History

The microprocessor was created in California in Silicon Valley. It was originally designed to meet the needs of a Japanese manufacturer of desktop calculators, the Nippon Calculating Machine Corporation. Intel[5] announced it commercially in an advertisement in the November 15, 1971, issue of Electronic News. In fact, this component was part of a family of four integrated circuits called MCS-4 (Intel 1973), MCS for Micro Computer Set. It consisted of the ROM with I/O port of 2 Kib, the RAM with output port of 320 bits, the SIPO register (Serial-In Parallel-Out) of 10 bits and the CPU referenced respectively 4001, 4002, 4003 and 4004. Originally, this company required the design of 12 integrated circuits for the Busicom 141-P calculating machine (Figure 1.1(a)). Marcian[6] E. Hoff, Jr., engineer in charge of the project at Intel, had the idea of integrating a programmable logic system. Subsequently, the rights were transferred to the company Intel for $60,000 at the time. The MPU included 2,300 transistors (Figure 1.1(b)), and it had a 4-bit architecture with single internal bus (*cf.* § V1-3.4.1). Ironically, the idea of the microprocessor was patented by the company Texas Instruments (Boone 1973). Additional historical information can be found in Noyce and Hoff (1981), Mazor (1995) and Halfhill (2006).

Before the microprocessor, there were several offers for the integration of logical subsets. Let us cite, in 1967, the company Fairchild which introduced a calculation unit in 8-bit format with an accumulator under the reference AL1. In 1969, the company Four Phased founded by Lee Boysel introduced a terminal using this component, perhaps the first bit-slice microprocessor (*cf.* § 5.1). In 1971, the offer revolved around families of components allowing realizing the function of MPU in discrete components. Let us take as an example of the MAPS family (Microprogrammable Arithmetic Processor System) from the company National Semiconductor (NS), which was a family of five components composed among others of an Arithmetic and Logic Unit (ALU) (MM5700), a register unit (MM5701), a control unit with a clock circuit (MM5702) and a control ROM (MM5705). In

---

5 The company Intel was founded on July 18, 1968, by Robert Noyce, Andy Grove and Gordon Moore, ex-employees of the company Fairchild, the latter not believing in the concept or unwilling to get started. Intel also designed the first RAM (Random Access Memory; *cf.* Chapter 4 of Darche (2012)) and the first EPROM (Erasable Programmable Read-Only Memory; this will be covered in a future book by the author on memories).

6 Nicknamed Ted.

addition, industrialists working for the American military worked on this type of family long before. Let us cite the D200 from Autonetics/North American Aviation (Booher 1968; Shirriff 2016).

a)   b)

Figure 1.1. *(a) The Busicom 141-P calculator and (b) photomicrograph of the 4004 (respective sources: Wikipedia.org and the Intel company). For a color version of this figure, see www.iste.co.uk/darche/microprocessor3.zip*

The next generation was the 8008, a component originally designed for the Datapoint 2200 terminal from Computer Terminal Corporation. The latter did not use it for performance reasons. It should be noted that the first MPU was the TMX 1795 (X for eXperimental) from the company TI, prototyped but never sold. The reference patent is Boone (1973). It was designed to replace the CPU of the Datapoint 2200 terminal. In 1972, the 8008 was used by the French company R2E to manufacture the first[7] microcomputer (MICRAL N released in 1973). This circuit manufactured in PMOS technology like its predecessor included 3,500 transistors. Its 8-bit architecture was single internal bus. The calculations despite its format were performed in n = 1 bit

---

7 Americans consider that the first microcomputer is American. It is the Altair 8800 from the American manufacturer MITS (Micro Instrumentation and Telemetry Systems), sold as a kit in 1975 (*cf.* § V1-1.2).

format. It was later followed by PPS-4 from Rockwell, PPS-25 from Fairchild, IMP-16[8] from NS and 5065 from Mostek.

To increase the speed of calculation, one approach has been to increase the format n of calculation. We also speak of bit-level parallelism. Thus, microprocessors can be classified into five generations by taking as a criterion the format of the integers that it handles. The first generation was that of 4 bits, then that of 8 bits, 16 bits and 8 bits improved, 32 bits and the fifth 64 bits. From the 16-bit generation, the components were called (at the time) "super microprocessor" (Vajda 1986) because they become able to execute programs written in High-Level programming Languages (HLL) and to support a multitasking Operating System (OS). Suzuoki *et al.* (1999) proposed a 128-bit version.

Table 1.1 presents two key characteristics of microprocessor development. The microprocessor now processes integers in 64-bit format when their format was originally 4 bits. The number of integrated transistors has increased from a few thousand to 10 billion. It thus doubled approximately every 18 months according to Moore's "law" allowing the integration of new functional units. Knowing that the acronyms CISC (Complex Instruction Set Computer) and RISC (Reduced Instruction Set Computer; this will be covered in a future book by the author on microprocessors) refer to models of ISA (Instruction Set Architecture, *cf.* § V1-3.5), it should be noted the downward difference in the number of transistors of this second architecture for a higher computing power. The economic aspect of the development of integrated circuits can be found in Moore (2003). In particular, it was found that the price of the transistor went from $1 in 1968 to 10^{-6} in 1998, a slope of about 37%/year.

Year of marketing	Company	Reference	Type	Format n bits of integer processing	Number of transistors
1971	Intel	4004	CISC	4	2,300 (2,238)
1972	Intel	8008	CISC	8	3,500
1974	Intel	4040	CISC	4	3,000
1974	Intel	8080	CISC	8	4,500
1974	Motorola	MC6800	CISC	8	4,100
1975	MOS Technology	MCS6502	CISC	8	4,528
1976	RCA	CDP1802	CISC	8	5,000

8 IMP for Integrated MicroProcessor, bit-slice version (*cf.* § 5.1).

1976	Intel	8085	CISC	8	6,500
1976	Zilog	Z80	CISC	8	8,500
1977	Motorola	MC6802	CISC	8	11,000
1978 (12/77)	Motorola	MC6809	CISC	8	9,000
1978	Intel	8086	CISC	16	29,000
1979	Intel	8088	CISC	16	29,000
1979	Zilog	Z8001	CISC	16	17,500
1979	Motorola	MC68000	CISC	16	68,000
1981	Intel	iAPX 432	CISC	32	97,000
1982	UC Berkeley	RISC I	RISC	32	44,420
1982	Intel	80186	CISC	16	55,000
1982	Intel	80286	CISC	16	134,000
1983	UC Berkeley	RISC II	RISC	32	40,760
1983	Stanford University	MIPS	RISC	32	24,000
1983	Zilog	Z80 000	CISC	32	91,000
1984	NS	NS32032	CISC	32	70,000
1984	Motorola	MC68020	CISC	32	190,000
1985	Intel	80386DX	CISC	32	275,000
1985	MIPS	R2000	RISC	32	110,000
1986	Fairchild Semiconductor	Clipper	RISC	32	300,000
1986	ARM	ARM1	RISC	32	24,800
1987	Motorola	MC68030	CISC	32	273,000
1987	ARM	ARM2	RISC	32	30,000
1988	MIPS	R3000	RISC	32	115,000
1988	Motorola	88100	RISC	32	165,000
1989	Intel	80486DX	CISC	32	1,180,235
1989	Intel	i860	RISC	32/64 (FPU)	$> 1 \times 10^6$

1991	Motorola	MC68040	CISC	32	1,200,000
1991	MIPS	R4000	RISC	64	1,350,000
1992	DEC	Alpha 21064	RISC	64	1,680,000
1993	Intel	Pentium	CISC	32	3,100,000
1993	HP	PA7100	RISC	32	850,000
1994	Motorola	MC68060	CISC	32	2,500,000
1995	Sun	UltraSPARC	RISC	64	5,200,000
1995	Intel	Pentium Pro	CISC	32	5,500,000
1996	AMD	K5	CISC	32	4,300,000
1997	Intel	Pentium II	CISC	32	7,500,000
1997	AMD	K6	CISC	32	8,800,000
1997	IBM-Motorola	PowerPC 750	RISC	32	6,350,000
1997	Sun	UltraSPARC II	RISC	64	5,400,000
1999	Intel	Pentium III	CISC	32	9,500,000
1999	AMD	Athlon	CISC	32	22×10^6
2000	Intel	Pentium 4 (Willamette)	CISC	32	42×10^6
2001	Sun	UltraSPARC III	RISC	64	29×10^6
2001	Intel	Itanium	EPIC[9]	64	25×10^6
2002	Intel	Itanium 2	EPIC	64	220×10^6
2002	Intel	Pentium 4 (Northwood)	CISC	32	55×10^6
2004	Intel	Pentium 4 (Prescott)	CISC	32	55×10^6
2005	Sun	UltraSPARC T1	RISC	64	279×10^6
2006	Intel	Core Duo	CISC	32	151×10^6
2006	Intel	Core 2 Duo	CISC	64	241×10^6

9 For Explicitly Parallel Instruction Computing (*cf.* § 4.7).

2006	Sony/IBM/Toshiba	Cell	RISC	64	234×10^6
2007	IBM	POWER6	RISC	64	790×10^6
2007	Sun	UltraSPARC T2	RISC	64	503×10^6
2008	Intel	Core i7 (4 cores)	CISC	64	731×10^6
2010	Sun/Oracle	SPARC T3 (16 cores)	RISC	64	1×10^9
2010	Intel	Core i7 (6 cores)	CISC	64	$1,17 \times 10^9$
2014	IBM	POWER8	RISC	64	$4,2 \times 10^9$
2015	Sun/Oracle	SPARC M7 (32 cores)	RISC	64	10×10^9

Table 1.1. *Number of transistors of the first microprocessors (Boland and Dollas (1994) completed)*

Another classification criterion was the complexity of the architecture. Thus, Tredennick (1996) offered the first generation, which was that of the first microprocessors with an operation according to the principles of von Neumann. The second generation introduced the pipeline (this will be covered in a future book by the author on microprocessors), the idea being to increase the bus occupancy rate by a functional division of the microprocessor. The 8088/8086 microprocessor had two functional units, the Execution Unit (EU) and the Bus Interface Unit (BIU). The third generation, in 1984, is that of the second-generation pipeline with the MC68020 (three-stage pipeline depth), which was the first MPU to introduce a cache. The fourth generation introduces the superscalar architecture of the 1990s. The fifth generation is that of current multicore chips with more than a billion transistors.

Since 1971, the year of its commercial announcement, the functionalities and the computing power (*cf.* § V4-3.4) of the microprocessor have not stopped increasing thanks to the progress of micro-electronic technologies. Its clock frequency went from 740 kHz (1971) to more than 3 GHz (2003) for a core, a factor of over 4,000 in 30 years (Table 1.2). Note that this parameter is an indicator of computing power (*cf.* § V4-3.4), but other parameters must be taken into account such as the number of cycles necessary to execute an instruction (*cf.* § 2.4.1) or the type of architecture (*cf.* § V1-3.1.4).

Year of sale	Company	Reference	Reference Internal clock frequency f (MHz) of the first version	Cycle time (ns) (= f^{-1})
1971	Intel	4004	740 kHz	1.35 µs
1972	Intel	8008	500 kHz	1.25 or 2 µs
1974	Intel	4040	740 kHz	1.35 µs
1974	Intel	8080	2	500
1974	Motorola	MC6800	1	1 µs
1975	MOS Technology	MCS6502	1	1 µs
1976	RCA	CDP1802	2.5 @ 5 V	400
1976	Intel	8085	3.125	320
1976	Zilog	Z80	2.5	400
1977	Motorola	MC6802	1	1 µs
1978 (12/77)	Motorola	MC6809	1	1 µs
1978	Intel	8086	5	200
1979	Intel	8088	5	200
1979	Zilog	Z8001	4	250
1979	Motorola	MC68000	8	125
1981	Intel	iAPX 432	5	200
1982	UC Berkeley	RISC I	1	1 µs
1982	Intel	80186	6	166
1982	Intel	80286	10	100
1983	UC Berkeley	RISC II	3	233
1983	Stanford University	MIPS	2	500
1983	Zilog	Z80 000	5	200
1984	NS	NS32032	10	100
1984	Motorola	MC68020	16	62.5
1985	Intel	80386DX	16	62.5
1985	MIPS	R2000	8	125
1986	Fairchild Semiconductor	Clipper	33	30
1986	ARM	ARM1	62	16.1
1987	Motorola	MC68030	20	50

1987	ARM	ARM2	8	125
1988	MIPS	R3000	12	83.3
1988	Motorola	88100	25	40
1989	Intel	80486DX	25	40
1989	Intel	i860	33	30
1991	Motorola	MC68040	25	40
1991	MIPS	R4000	100	10
1992	DEC	Alpha 21064	150	6.66
1993	Intel	Pentium	66	15
1993	HP	PA7100	100	10
1994	Motorola	MC68060	50	20
1995	Sun	UltraSPARC	143	6.99
1995	Intel	Pentium Pro	150	6.66
1996	AMD	K5	75	13.3
1997	Intel	Pentium II	233	4.29
1997	AMD	K6	166	6.02
1997	IBM-Motorola	PowerPC 750	233	4.29
1997	Sun	UltraSPARC II	200	5
1999	Intel	Pentium III	450	2.22
1999	AMD	Athlon	500	2
2000	Intel	Pentium 4 (Willamette)	1,300	0.77
2001	Sun	UltraSPARC III	600	1.66
2001	Intel	Itanium	733	1.36
2002	Intel	Itanium 2	1,000	1
2002	Intel	Pentium 4 (Northwood)	1,300	0.77
2004	Intel	Pentium 4 (Prescott)	3,400	0.29
2005	Sun	UltraSPARC T1	1,200	0.833
2006	Intel	Core Duo	1,100	0.90
2006	Intel	Core 2 Duo	1,860	0.54
2006	Sony/IBM/Toshiba	Cell	3,200	0.313

2007	IBM	POWER6	3,600	0.28
2007	Sun	UltraSPARC T2	1,400	0.71
2008	Intel	Core i7 (4 cores)	2,660	0.38
2010	Sun/Oracle	SPARC T3 (16 cores)	1,600	0.625
2010	Intel	Core i7 (6 cores)	3,200	0.31
2014	IBM	POWER8	3,000	0.33
2015	Sun/Oracle	SPARC M7 (32 cores)	4,130	0.242

Table 1.2. *Frequency of first microprocessors (Boland and Dollas (1994) completed)*

The dotted line in Figure 1.2 indicates the break introduced by the introduction of multicore in order to stop the increase in the operating frequency. By refining, Hennessy and Patterson (2011) calculated three growth rates, 15%/year (1978–1986), then 40% (1986–2003) and, finally, less than 1%/year (2003–2010). The last level does not mean a stagnation in performance, but it corresponds to the transition to multicore architecture, the frequency of a core no longer increasing among other things for reasons of energy dissipation (*cf.* § 6.1.2). In addition, computing power (unit of measurement: MIPS for Million Instructions Per Second; *cf.* § V4-3.4.2) increases by about 40% per year. The red brick wall symbolizes the physical limit to integration and, perhaps, that of computing power.

As illustrated in Figure V1-1.15, microelectronic technology for manufacturing integrated circuits has evolved over time. Initially of the bipolar type, it slowly evolved towards unipolar technologies, MOS then, today, CMOS. The first microprocessors were manufactured in unipolar PMOS technologies and NMOS (negative (channel) MOS) for reasons of switching speed and number of supply voltages. The tables in Chapter 4 indicate the technologies of these first components. In addition, these technological advances will have an impact on the value of the supply voltage (Figure 6.1) and on current consumption. Bipolar technology was only reserved for areas where speed of calculation was essential, such as the military with its real-time and signal processing applications. Let us cite as examples of this component the SBP9989 (Lucas and Sobering 1983) and the F9450, manufactured in the following technologies respectively I^2L (Integrated Injection Logic; *cf.* § 2.3.2 of Darche (2004)) and I^3L (Isoplanar I^2L (Hennig *et al.* (1977)), which were 16-bit models from TI and NS respectively. The bit-slice processors (*cf.* § 5.1) were also mainly manufactured in bipolar technology for the same reason.

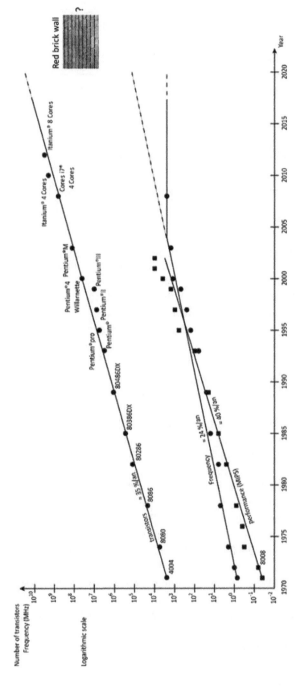

Figure 1.2. Evolution over time of the internal clock frequency and the number of transistors for the Intel range. For a color version of this figure, see www.iste.co.uk/darche/microprocessor3.zip

Figure 1.3 shows the classification of the first microprocessors on the market. The dotted line indicates a break in characteristics (set of instructions not compatible; *cf.* § V4-3.3.2). A microprocessor can belong to a family, for example, x86, MIPS or SPARC. This notion was introduced by Stevens (1964) who defined it as a set of processor implementations, each of which, capable of executing programs written for others. As for the classes of Bell (2008a, 2008b) (*cf.* § V1-1.2), these processors belong in the same price and performance category. The interest for the user lies in the fact that he can migrate to a more efficient machine of the family while keeping compatibility. For a microprocessor, this means that it shares a set of characteristics such as a base instruction set (i.e. basic) allowing, for example, a backward compatibility (*cf.* § V4-3.3.3) of the programs. A generation manipulates the same data format. The 8-bit generation (*cf.* § 4.3) can be broken down into three phases, the first with the 8008, the second with the 8080 and the MC6800 and the MCS6502 and the third with the 8085, the MC6802 and the Z80. The representatives of the 16-bit generation microprocessors (*cf.* § 4.5) were the MC68000 from Motorola, the Z8001 from Zilog and, of course, the 8086[10] from Intel. They are compared in Heering (1980). What characterizes the 16-bit generation is the introduction of advanced memory management (i.e. virtual memory; this will be covered in a future book by the author on microprocessors), a set of instructions and advanced addressing modes and parallelism (Whitworth 1980). To this list, we must add the introduction of several execution modes, mainly user and supervisor modes (*cf.* § V4-3.2.2). Virtual memory with its segmentation and paging mechanisms introduces a logical address space (*cf.* § 2.1.1.1) for the more important programmer, protecting memory and relocating code and data. The 1980s saw the emergence of multiprocessor systems. This generation undoubtedly marks the decline of Assembly Language (AL) in favor of High-Level programming Languages (HLL). The 32-bit generation (*cf.* § 4.6) appeared with the MC68020 from Motorola in 1984. The 64-bit generation (*cf.* § 4.7) appeared in 1991 with the R4000, which had a RISC architecture (this will be covered in a future book by the author on microprocessors). IEEE (1996) presents testimonies of the stakeholders of this history. Its new integrated features allow the operating system architecture to evolve and speed up its operation.

In the beginning, the designer and manufacturer of a microprocessor were identical with, possibly, one or more second sources that manufactured the component under license. Take as an example the circuit referenced MC6809 whose designer and manufacturer was Motorola. There were also second sources such as the French EFCIS (company which later became SGS-Thomson Microelectronics, then STMicroelectronics), AMI (American Microsystems, Inc.), Fairchild and Hitachi. Today, they can be separate, as is the case for the Arm® processor (Advanced RISC Machines) that the company of the same name, without factory (fabless), licenses to manufacturers in the form of Intellectual Property (IP) that is, a reusable and

---

10 It should be noted that the object code of 8085 was not compatible with that of 8088/86.

configurable basic brick. We must thus distinguish three trades, which consist of designing the IP block in itself that which consists of designing a SoC based on IP blocks and that which is in charge of manufacturing (the founder). Thus, companies only design components (MIPS as another example), others manufacture the component like any other integrated circuit and, finally, companies design and manufacture (designers and founders like Intel, for example). There may also be components from competing companies compatible in terms of hardware and/or software (*cf.* § V4-3.3), Table 1.3 showing an example with the x86 family. Competitors in this family at the time included the companies Cyrix, AMD and Nec. As a complement, Hennessy (1984) details the architecture of the VLSI (Very LSI) microprocessors.

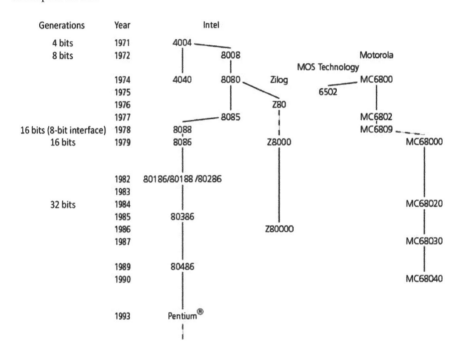

Figure 1.3. *Examples of classification of the first main families of microprocessors (RISC families excluded)*

Alternative source type	Development required	AMD x86 CPU generation
Second source license	Manufacturing only	8086 and 80286
Unlicensed CPU clone	Reverse engineering	386 and 486
CPU-compatible at pin level	Original CPU design (parallel engineering)	K5 (with *chipset* Pentium)
Software-compatible CPU	Original CPU and chipset designs	K6 and K7
Upward-compatible CPU	Original 64-bit CPU and chipset designs	K8

Table 1.3. *Hardware and software compatibilities for the x86 family (Halfhill 2009)*

1.3. Conclusion

This chapter presented a brief history of the development of microprocessors by specifying, in particular the different generations of components.

Microprocessor Interfacing

Interfacing concerns the interconnection of the MPU (MicroProcessor Unit) with external logical components or units. This mainly concerns the memory and the Input/Output controllers (I/O). This set communicates by buses (*cf.* the previous volume). The type of architecture will have a consequence on their number and on the organization of the memory or memories; in particular, in the Harvard architecture (*cf.* § V1-3.4.2), the instructions will be stored in memory separately from the data (separate addressing plans) or not.

The designer must adapt the interface signals of the interconnected components. Like all logic signals, these are characterized temporally and electrically for this purpose. These characteristics depend on the implementation logic; today we mainly have the CMOS (Complementary Metal-Oxide Semiconductor) technology. The designer must refer to the manufacturer's datasheet (*cf.* Chapter 6) to consult the latter. But before studying the interface of the microprocessor with its external environment, reminders on the buses and on the peripheral logic to the microprocessor are made.

2.1. Microprocessor bus

Figure 2.1 shows the component in situation. The operation is of Master–Slaves type (M/S) with the microprocessor being always the master of exchanges. In other configurations, such as a system whose exchanges will be made by DMA (Direct Memory Access, *cf.* § 4.1.3 of Darche (2003)) or a multiprocessor system, control of exchanges may be shared between several bus masters. We find the classic bus for addresses (address bus), data (data bus) and control (control bus) respectively of width m, n and c. For educational purposes, they will be considered as not multiplexed (*cf.* § V2-1.1). These buses can be qualified as sub-buses when they are part of a higher-level bus such as a local bus (*cf.* § V2-4.2.1). All the signals coming from the buses are amplified by electronic buffers or drivers (not shown), which thus isolate the nodes from the buses. These buffers are now integrated into the components. The same goes for outgoing signals whose associated buffers are generally of the three-state[1] type (three-state logic, *cf.* interfacing logic, § 2.2.1 and 3.4.2 of Darche (2004)). Note that in the early days, a processor could require peripheral[2] logic circuits such as a clock circuit or a bus controller such as, for example, the circuit referenced 8228 from Intel. McKenzie (1976) gives an example of design. In addition, examples of evaluation boards (*cf.* § V5-2.1.1) with this organization are presented in Intel (1981).

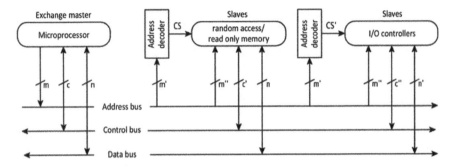

Figure 2.1. *A simple microprocessor system*

2.1.1. *Address bus*

The MPU addresses the slave components, that is, the main memory and the I/O controllers, via the associated buses using an address decoding system. Recall that an address is a numerical designation (i.e. a natural or relative whole number) of a location or cell for a memory. Those that are carried on this bus are physical addresses as opposed to virtual addresses since they are intended for hardware components. The address bus in format m consists of wires A_0 to A_{m-1} (also noted A[m-1:0]). Another designation of its signals can give information to the electronics engineer. For example, AD (Address/Data) means that it is a multiplexed bus (in time).

2.1.1.1. *Address space*

The Address Space (AS) is the set of possible addresses that can travel on the address bus. For a processor, this is therefore the set of addresses that it can generate. Its size therefore depends on the format of its ordinal counter (*cf.* § 3.1.3). The format or number of address wires generally determines its space or its address capacity C ($C = 2^m$ in the case of a non-multiplexed bus (*cf.* § V2-1.2)). For a bus, it is therefore a

---

1 TRI-STATE® is a registered trademark of National Semiconductor.

2 In the sense of "around" and not in the sense of "I/O hardware".

function of its width w. Its range C is given by the formula [2.1]. Note that an additional address bit is required every 18 months (Gray and Shenay 1999). Address resolution is the smallest amount of addressable information.

$$C = 2^w \qquad\qquad\qquad\qquad [2.1]$$

Let us recall three addressing capacities as a time reference, that of the IBM 701 scientific computer (1952 or 1953), which was 2 Ki words of 36 bits; that of the PDP-8 mini-computer from the company Digital Equipment Corporation or DEC (1965) of 4 Ki words of 12 bits and that of the MC6800 component of 64 Ki words of 8 bits. These are the weak memory capacities of the time, which motivated the invention of the concept of virtual memory (this will be covered in a future book by the author on memories). This space can be divided into blocks of fixed size called "page" for reasons of speed of memory access. These pages are numbered from 0. For 8-bit microprocessors (cf. § 4.3), their size is 256 addresses (= 2^8). This means that the 8 least significant bits of the address bus address the content of a page. Historically, the physical addressing capacity of microprocessors originally went from 4 Ki × 4 (4004) to 512 GiB (address format m = 39 bits, eighth-generation Intel Core) today.

Note that the address space can be continuous or discontinuous. Depending on the processor architecture, there may be multiple AS that can be separated logically or physically. In the latter case, each AS is characterized by separate communication channels, which offers better access performance and greater flexibility in design. Bus formats can be different. A first example is the Harvard architecture (cf. § V1-3.4.2), which is distinguished by differentiated AS for code and data. A second example is I/O where there are going to be two input/output management philosophies with the microprocessor manufacturers which we name "Motorola philosophy" and "Intel philosophy" (cf. § 2.3 of (Darche 2003). The first consists of mixing the memory addresses and those of input–output (Figure 2.2(a)) hence the name, Memory-Mapped I/O (MMIO). The I/O space is in fact the memory space. The instruction set associated with the management is said to be trivialized because it is the same as accessing memory or a register of a controller. The fact of not differentiating memory addresses from I/O addresses simplifies the hardware (HW). There are no specific I/O control signals simplifying interfacing. They benefit from the full set of instructions (cf. Chapter V4-2). Sometimes the controller can benefit from faster access as proposed by the MC6800 with direct addressing (cf. § V4-1.2.3.1). DMA-type transfer (cf. § 1.2 and 4.1.3 of Darche (2003)) is made easier because the memory space is unique. The second approach is to separate the memory plane from the addressing plane of the input–output circuits (Figure 2.2(b)). The approach is called separate or Isolated I/O (IIO) or I/O per port (I/O port). The I/O address space and memory are separate and independent. A memory in the I/O space is called I/O memory, which should not be confused with the main memory. Accessing independent address, data, code and I/O spaces requires specific control signals. For example, there will be separate read/write signals for memory and I/O. For transfers, it is also necessary to have a specialized and limited instruction set. Let us cite, for example, in and out instructions in the case of an Intel x86 processor or, for the Zilog company, more advanced ones which perform auto-increment or auto-decrement, ini(r) (*in/increment/repeat*), ind(r) (in/*decrement/repeat*), outi *(OUT/Increment)*, otir (OuT/*Increment/Repeat*), outd *(OUT/Decrement)*, otdr *(OuT/Decrement/Repeat)*. The execution of these specialized instructions activates dedicated access signals, and a specific bus accesses the registers. This results in an increase in the address space. The I/O space is generally smaller (256 ports in general, p = 8). On the other hand, additional instructions complicate the microprocessor control unit, but access to the inputs–outputs is better protected because the specialized instructions are generally executed in protected or privileged mode (*cf.* § V4-3.2.2). The electronics engineer can, at the cost of a complication of the glue (i.e. peripheral logic, *cf.* § 2.3), switch from an operation with separate I/O to a single address space. Address decoding is more complex because it is necessary to take into account the signals specialized in I/O accesses. The advantage is the increase in the size of the I/O space, which is generally smaller than that of the memory addresses. The reverse passage is however impossible.

A special case of exchange with the I/O address space to note is that of the TMS 9900 from Texas Instruments. In fact, the address is sent conventionally by the 12 bits of the address bus, but the data exchange takes place serially using a special register, CRU (Communication Register Unit) and of three signals CRUIn, CROut and CRUClk (TI 1976).

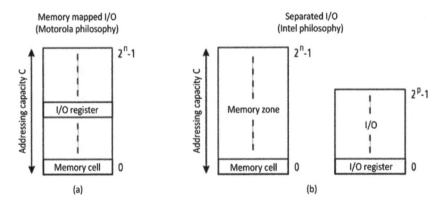

Figure 2.2. *Two possible input–output managements*

There is also a third type of address space dedicated to the management of a bus. It is named Configuration Space or Control and Status Register (CSR) space or, simply, control space (Figure 2.3(c)). It is specific to each card. These CSRs are initialized at system startup. This AS allows the MPU to access the configuration registers of the entities of an advanced extension bus such as the PCI bus (Peripheral Component Interconnect, *cf.* § V2-4.2.4). The addresses of this space are obviously independent of the two other spaces, of memory and I/O respectively represented by the Figures 2.3(a) and (b). An example of standardization of this type of registers can be found in IEEE (2002c).

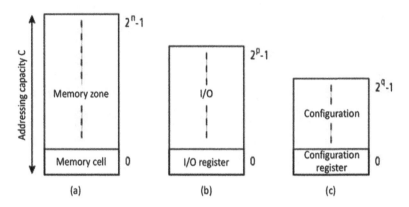

Figure 2.3. *Three separate address plans of (a) memory, (b) I/O and (c) configuration*

A storage space is not necessarily an address space. For example, from a programmer's perspective, the registers on a microprocessor do not have an address. Some authors like Van de Goor (1989) speak of register space or working storage. We are rather talking about a namespace since each of it has a symbolic name in the ISA (Instruction Set Architecture, *cf.* § V1-3.5) and which can be used in assembly language (*cf.* § V5-1.3). Another case is the stack (*cf.* § V4-4.1) which is a storage space (stack space) accessible to the programmer without address. In addition, geographic addressing (*cf.* § V2-1.5) allows the position of the element in the bus to be taken into account. All these spaces are accessible to the programmer via the assembly language (*cf.* § V5-1.3.5).

These AS may or may not correspond to one or more addressing modes of the MPU, subject to § V4-1.2.

2.1.1.2. *Address decoding*

Address decoding was studied in Darche (2003, 2012). From the address, a slave circuit among all the addressable elements is selected from the address generated by the microprocessor by activating one or more selection signals CS (Chip Select) or CE

(Chip Enable). Also remember that the decoding can be linear or not, complete (or exhaustive) or incomplete (or partial). Linear decoding means that the Integrated Circuit (IC) packages are selected directly using the address wires. The address space (*cf.* subsection below) is partitioned into ranges, each of which is assigned to a subset or component addressed. More conventionally, a decoding logic is responsible for the selection of the latter. If the decoding is not complete, ghost addresses may appear. This last aspect as well as the logical decoding solutions applied to I/O interfaces but transposable to any other addressable component were studied in § 2.2.2 of Darche (2003).

2.1.1.3. *Memory expansion*

The paging technique can also be used (*cf.* § V5-3.2.3 for an industrial example). Memory expansion techniques allow a processor to expand its memory size beyond the maximum limit without changing its initial addressing capacity. They are mainly used by microcontrollers (*cf.* § 5.3) which have a limited number of address lines. The latter use their I/O lines to switch memory banks[3]. The paging technique can also be used (*cf.* § V5-3.2.3 for an industrial example).

2.1.1.4. *Multiple access*

The access to a memory word can be done in several access cycles if it is not framed in the memory format (i.e. alignment, *cf.* § V1-1.2 and § 2.6.1 of Darche (2012)). Access to memory can also be done according to a sub-multiple of n. For example, it can be a 1-byte access while the memory is organized in 16-bit words. The interest is to be able to manage in memory words of different sizes, multiple of the byte in general. It is necessary to have one or more additional signals which participate in address decoding. Let us quote, for example, the signals #UDS and #LDS (Upper/Lower Data Strobe, *cf.* § V2-1.5 to observe them in use) from MC68000 from Motorola or the signal BHE (Bus High Enable) from 8086 from Intel.

2.1.2. *Data bus*

The data bus[4] in format n is designated by wires D_0 to D_{n-1}. The number of bits n generally indicates the processing format of the integers of the central unit in the case of a non-multiplexed bus. The width is often a multiple of the byte with exceptions such as the IMS6100 of the company Intersil with instruction set compatible with the

---

3 This concept has been addressed in the internal organization of memories (*cf.* § 2.3.1 and 2.3.2 of Darche (2012)).

4 It should be noted that the data bus carries information in the broad sense, that is, the instruction codes (*cf.* § V4-1.1) of the programs and also data and addresses (a pointer for example).

PDP-8 with a format n of 12 bits (Thomas 1976) and MC14500B (n = 1) of the Motorola company. However, a processor can process data of much larger size than that transported by the data bus for economic reasons (*cf.* § V2-1.1). In the last case (multiplexed bus), the number of information bits must be totaled. An example is that of the company Intel, which proposed two versions of the same 16-bit core: 8088 and 8086. The former exchanged this data on the data bus in the form of two bytes, while the latter, in a single operation, on 16 bits. An MPU can have a bus with a format twice that of the data to be processed to double the data rate and increase the instruction rate with the notion of instruction packet (instruction bundle). An example is the Itanium (IA-64 architecture) with a 128-bit wide bus, twice its working format, each instruction word containing three instruction codes (Liu *et al.* 2006).

2.1.3. *Control bus*

The essential signals of the control bus are the timing signals of the exchanges or of the clock (classic name: E or Clk) if the dialogue is synchronous, the synchronization signal(s) (Strobe and Ack, for example) and the type of access. The latter indicates whether the exchange is a read or a write. It requires either two separate Read/#Write signals[5] (this is the approach from Intel with the 8080 microprocessor) or a single signal (classic name: Read/#Write or R/#W for short) since the type of access is exclusive (this is the approach of Motorola with the MC6800 microprocessor). There may be a specific read/write signal for I/O (I/O read and write) if there are separate address spaces.

The other signal families are used to manage the bus. We can cite the request, authorization, occupation and possibly bus release signals (*cf.* § V2-1.6) and DMA (Direct Memory Access) type transfers. There are also the hardware trap signals (*cf.* § V4-5.2) like the maskable (e.g. #INT) and non-maskable interrupt trap signals (e.g. #NMI for Non-Maskable Interrupt) and the signal initialization (e.g. #Reset). There are other less common signals such as a processor stop signal (#HALT), which requests an interruption.

2.2. Hardware interface

At the hardware level, these are the signals from the microprocessor (Figure 2.4). We also talk about the system interface. We find the signals of the address, data and

---

5 The # symbol, preferred in this work, indicates an activation of the signal in the low state (*cf.* § 3.2 of Darche (2012)). Other symbols can be encountered, such as the minus sign or the slash in prefix or suffix, the prefix Not or even the complementation bar on the name of the symbol.

control buses, in particular for memory access (R/#WE signal for example). The designer must ensure electrical compatibility between these signals and those of the components connected to them. The connection can be direct or be made using auxiliary components in parallel such as, for example, a simple pull-up resistor (*cf.* § 2.1.1 of Darche (2004)), or in series, for example, an active component such as the level shifter (*cf.* § 3.8.2 of Darche (2004)) or a passive component such as an impedance matching resistance. Compatibility must also be logical with signals which can be a combinatorial or even sequential logical function (*cf.* Chapters 2 and 3 of Darche (2002)) of other signals. The power pins have not been specified in this figure. Clock signals are generated internally from a signal or an external component like, here, quartz Q.

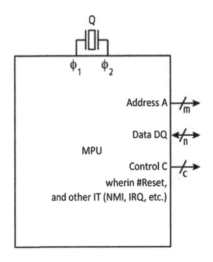

Figure 2.4. *Classic interface signals*

2.3. Peripheral logic

The Anglo-Saxon term glue logic, which can be translated literally as "sticky logic", is a generic term which designates a set of logical operators (GPL for General-Purpose Logic) which are combinatorial (most of the time) and sequential, which achieves a very specific function, for example, here address decoding or storage (latch function) around a component or a unit (respectively *cf.* § 2.2.2 of Darche (2003), § 2.2.6 of Darche (2012) and § 3.4.3 of Darche (2002)). When a microprocessor or a controller integrates it, it is said to be glueless, that is, there is no longer any need for this external logic since it is integrated. The interest lies in the simplification of the design and the increased reliability of the electronics. An introduction can be found in

Nicoud (1991). Other functions are the electrical adaptation of signals (at the electrical or temporal level) and the conversion of protocols (*cf.* § V2-4.1.4).

2.4. Temporal aspects

The logic components are characterized temporally (*cf.* § 1.3 of Darche (2004)) for a temperature range (conventionally at least three: commercial, industrial and military) and a range of the supply voltage(s). When their operation is synchronous, one or more clocks provide the main timing signals. The exchange protocol is described in the sheet of characteristics (datasheet, *cf.* Chapter 6) in the form of chronograms (*cf.* § 3.3.1 of Darche (2012)) associated with tables of temporal characteristics of the signals represented.

2.4.1. *Clock*

The clock signal generator is the electronic component or unit responsible for generating the clock signal(s), time reference(s) of the logic system. It is called clock source because of its function. A clock signal is a periodic logic signal which rates or synchronizes the operation of a circuit or a system, here logical (Figure 2.5), for example, a microprocessor, a synchronous memory or an I/O controller. For this, a component, a quartz (crystal) Q generally or a ceramic or surface acoustic wave resonator (SAW for Surface Acoustic Wave), an RC phase shifter network (Resistor–Capacitor) or an LC resonant circuit (inductor L – Capacitor) is used by the oscillating circuit to generate this signal. The assembly can be integrated into an external package to the MPU for reasons of precision and frequency stability. This independent source of clock called oscillator can be associated with electronics to generate all the signals of the subsets of the system like the buses, the memory and the processors. The output of the oscillator ϕ_i ($I \in [0, h\text{-}1]$, $h \in \mathbb{N}^*$) can be of the unipolar type, but today, with high clocking frequencies (order of magnitude $f > 100$ MHz), it is differential.

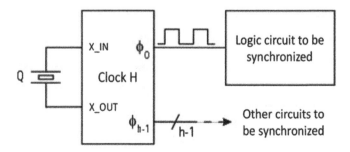

Figure 2.5. *Clock circuits external to the microprocessor*

A classic intermediate solution is to leave the aforementioned resonant component outside and integrate the rest of the oscillator, as shown in Figure 2.6. It is thus possible to choose its frequency by the choice of quartz, or even to use anyway an external oscillator if the designer wishes it as suggested by the name of the MPU signals knowing that the clock signal comes out by Osc_Out. The RC network-based solution is an economical but not frequency-stable solution reserved for low-end digital systems such as electronic toys. Note that the outgoing clock signals are buffered, that is, electrically amplified (see below).

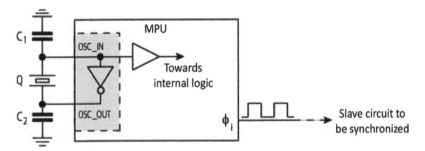

Figure 2.6. *Internal clock circuits of the microprocessor*

The first microprocessors (8008, 8080, MC6800) required multiple clock signals and their generation was complex, as shown in the example in Figure 2.7. This is a two-phase non-overlapping clocks version, the signals being of negative logic type (*cf.* § 2.1.4 of Darche (2004)). A third synchronization output signal called Sync indicates the start of an instruction cycle. An external clock circuit like the MC6875 for the MC6800 was responsible for generating them. Note that the manufacturer can specify a minimum frequency as for the MC6800. This indicates that the internal logic is then of the dynamic type.

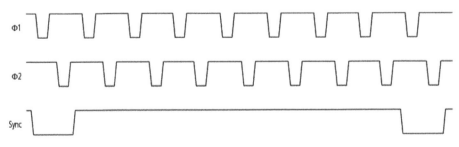

Figure 2.7. *Complex clock signals and synchronization signal of the first microprocessor referenced 4004*

Figure 2.8 shows the clock signals of the PPS-4. Each state of signal $\bar{B}$ will be an internal state (*cf.* § 3.4.1) of the machine representing a cycle $\phi 1$ to $\phi 4$. It should be noted that the frequency of $\bar{B}$ is twice the first.

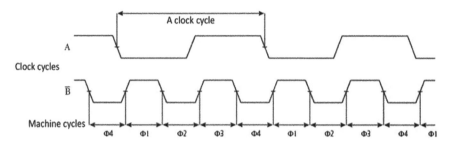

Figure 2.8. *Correspondence between clock cycle and machine cycles for the PPS-4*

The clock signals of 8008 (Figure 2.9) are of the positive logic type (*cf.* § 2.1.4 of Darche (2004)). The Sync signal, whose frequency is half that of the ϕi signals, is used to indicate cycle 0 to the external logic.

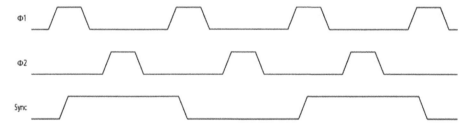

Figure 2.9. *8008 microprocessor complex clock signals*

We can deduce that the execution of an instruction is done in an instruction cycle. This consists of several machine cycles, each of which is made up of one or more clock periods (Figure 2.10). A T-state corresponds to a period of the internal clock which cadences the operation of the MPU. It is a subdivision of an execution cycle. The number of T-states can be variable, depending on the component. Figure 2.10 breaks down an instruction cycle into sub-cycles and T-state. Formally, each machine cycle has several states. The concept of state is formalized by the concept of state machine or FSM for Finite-State Machine, which is a formal model, that is, an abstraction.

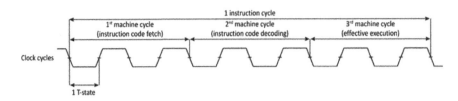

Figure 2.10. *Breakdown of the execution of an instruction into machine cycles*

Figure 2.11 shows decompositions of some iconic 8-bit MPUs. It should be noted that the number of machine cycles, as well as the number of states can be fixed or variable.

The time characteristics in addition to the input and output frequencies specify the quality of the signal(s). Let us cite the jitter(s) (unit: fs or ps), the propagation delay (unit: ns) and the output skew (unit: ps). Explanations of the temporal characteristics of the signals are found in § 3.3 of Darche (2012). Let us cite the rise time t_r (rise time) and fall time t_f (fall time), those in high and low states, the different phase shifts and the duty cycle. The two-phase signals are generally in phase opposition, each of them having a duty cycle of 1/2 easier to generate using, for example, a D Flip-Flop (*cf.* FF, § 3.4.3 of Darche (2002)). On the other hand, the worst time case is always represented as shown in Figure 2.12. For $\phi 1$, the rise and fall times respectively t_{TLHM} and t_{THLM}, and the duration of the pulse t_{PWM}, as well as the phase shift between the two signals t_{PLHM} (minimum 0 ns) are specified. The other times have not been reproduced so as not to overload the illustration.

Designing a clock system becomes more complicated with increasing frequency. The paths of this type of signal are crucial. It is necessary to guarantee the temporal characteristics of these signals such as, for example, the same propagation time regardless of the position on the chip of the logic systems using them. More details of clock path design are given in Wagner (1988). Because of the speed of propagation (order of magnitude externally: 15 cm/ns for a transmission line (*cf.* § V2-3.3.1) of an FR4-type Printed Circuit Board (PCB)) and their high frequency, there will be logical subsets that will operate at different frequencies. These zones are called "Clock Domain" or CD (*cf.* § 3.6.6 of Darche (2012)). When there is communication between these zones, electronic problems such as metastability appear (*cf.* § 3.5.2 of Darche (2004)), which must be resolved.

Also, in addition to this main signal generation function, its additional functions are fan-out amplification, jitter cleaning, frequency multiplication or division and frequency synthesis.

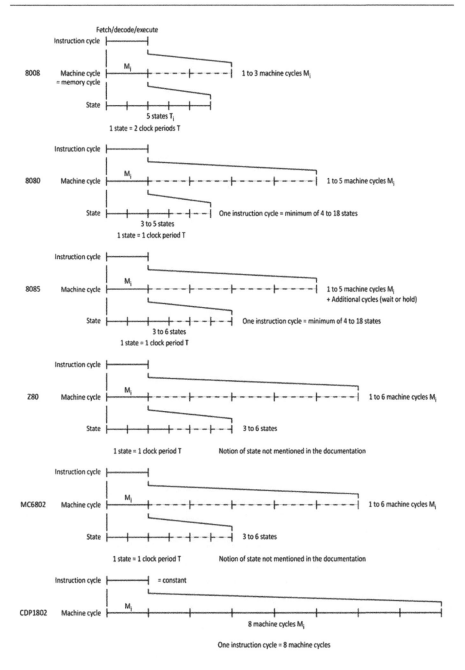

Figure 2.11. *Temporal breakdown of an instructional cycle in machine cycles and 8-bit generation MPU states*

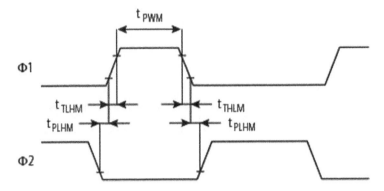

Figure 2.12. *MC6800 microprocessor complex clock signals*

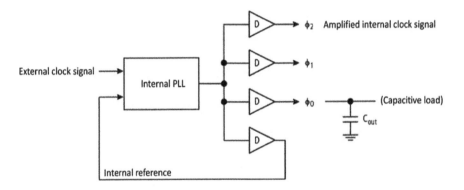

Figure 2.13. *Delay-locked loop in a processor*

All these functions use the Phase-Locked Loop (PLL, *cf.* § 2.2.10 of Darche (2012)). A PLL performs the basic functions which are the elimination of the propagation times linked to the dispersion of the characteristics between buffers, the adjustment of the phase, the correction of the duty cycle, the elimination of the clock jitter and the synthesis frequency by performing a division or a multiplication, whole or fractional, of a reference signal. The signal is amplified using an electronic buffer D called a driver or fan-out buffer (*cf.* § 3.4.1 of Darche (2004)), as illustrated in Figure 2.13. They are necessary to operate on highly capacitive bus lines or for signals with high entrance (*cf.* § 2.2.1 of Darche (2004)). For modern microprocessors (release date greater than 1988), as the frequency increases, above ten MHz, the propagation time and the time shift (*skew*) between the external and internal clock signals generated by the line amplifiers must be reduced. The use of a PLL upstream of the output buffers with a feedback of an output of one of these buffers to one of its comparison inputs makes it possible to resolve the problems of phase shift between the different outputs.

Frequency division can be done using a counter (*cf.* § 3.5.6 of Darche (2002)) in the simplest case or a PLL. The latter is then associated with frequency predivisors (prescaling). Thus associated, it also makes it possible to carry out frequency multiplication. These two operations can be whole or fractional. Figure 2.14 illustrates the point, the position of the predivisor varying according to the requested function.

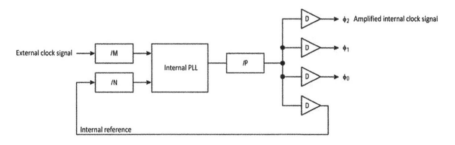

Figure 2.14. *PLL-based divider/multiplier*

Quartz oscillators generally operate in fundamental mode, which limits their frequency. To obtain a higher frequency, it is necessary to use another so-called partial oscillation mode (overtone) for the 100 MHz or a frequency multiplier to go up in the GHz range. Also associated with the external clock, the phase-locked loop internally provides a signal with a frequency multiple of that of a reference signal and in phase. Young *et al.* (1992) gives an example of design. A Delay-Locked Loop (DLL, *cf.* § 2.2.11 of Darche (2012)) can also be used. These circuits allow programming of the multiplier factor via, for example, the BIOS (Basic Input/Output System, *cf.* § V5-3.5.3 and Chapter 4 of Darche (2003)). Finally, a PLL associated with a VCXO (Voltage-Controlled Crystal Oscillator) can suppress the jitter (*cf.* § 3.5.3 of Darche (2004) and *cf.* § 7.1.2 of Darche (2012)) of a signal output relative to a reference input signal (jitter cleaning). In current MPUs, several clock signals with different but not necessarily multiple frequencies must be generated. Several PLLs must then be used (Figure 2.15).

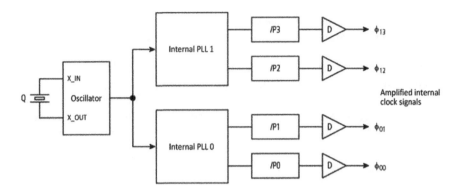

Figure 2.15. *Frequency synthesizer using PLL*

A modern oscillator follows the technical time and electrical recommendations of the manufacturer. For Intel, these are, for example, recommendations CK97, CK98, CK00, CK409, CK410B/B +, CK420BQ/BQL or CK505. It generates all the reference time signals for the subsets of a digital system which are the MPU(s), the (synchronous) Random Access Memory (RAM), the system and extension bus(es) and the chipsets (*cf.* § V5-3.3). Its outputs are unipolar or differential. The solutions proposed are for one (Figure 2.16) or two circuits. In the latter case, the second contains the majority of the line drivers (*cf.*, for example, the recommendation DB800 (DB for Differential Buffer) or DB1200 from the company Intel).

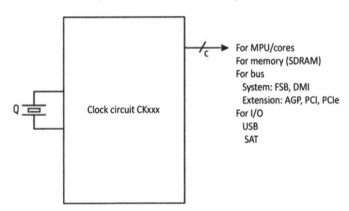

Figure 2.16. *Modern clock circuit (single-circuit solution) at Intel*

Overclocking is a technique that involves increasing the operating frequency of a logic system to increase the operating speed and, therefore, its performance. The physical consequences are increased electrical consumption (*cf.* § 6.1.2) and, above all, an increase in temperature, which risks destroying the components if suitable cooling is not implemented. A technique used by video game players at first for the MPU and then today for the GPU (Graphics Processing Unit), it is also used for industrialists.

Figure 2.17 shows a model of the clock system of an MPU. The frequency of the external oscillator is not necessarily the internal frequency of the processor. It can be divided or multiplied by a factor k' (natural integer k', but this is no longer an obligation today). An example is the MC680x microprocessor from Motorola, whose oscillator frequency was 4 MHz. The latter is then divided by a factor k = 4 to give the internal reference frequency for calculating the cycle time of signal E. Another example is the 8085 whose input frequency is divided by 2. Another example from Intel is a unique BCLK (Bus CLocK) signal which controls the speed of operation of the external bus, qualified as frontal or FSB (Front-Side Bus) and that of the cores. The multiplication ratios are fixed at manufacture, adjusted materially by external signals or programmed via a value stored in a control register. The front bus/core frequency ratios for the first Pentiums (microarchitecture P5) were 1:1, 1:3, 2:5, 1:2 and 2:3 (factor k:p ≤ 1, with f_{BCLK} = 66.66 MHz = constant). Another example of ratios varying from 1/17 to 1/22 concerned the Xeon® MP varying its internal frequency from 2.83 to 3.66 GHz (f_{BCLK} = 166 MHz).

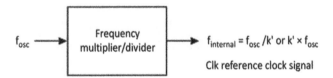

Figure 2.17. *Relationship between clock signals*

From the oscillator clock period T_{osc}, the basic cycle time t_{cycle_clock} (unit: seconds), the period of the reference clock signal Clk, is defined. Assuming that k' ≤ 1 and that the clock module acts as a divider, the relationship between them is as follows:

$$t_{clock\_cycle} = \frac{T_{osc}}{k'} \qquad [2.2]$$

The cycle time t_{clock_cycle} is the time reference for operating the MPU. This clock cycle is a clock period during which a micro-operation (i.e. internal operation) is carried out, hence the name of cycle time (of the machine $t_{machine\_cycle}$. It is a discrete time interval. There will then exist two families of processors, those whose execution cycle of an instruction (*cf.* § V1-3.2.2.4 and V1-3.3.2) requires a clock cycle (single (clock)-cycle instruction execution) and those that need multiple cycles (multi-cycle instruction execution or multiple (clock)-cycle instruction execution). This basic execution time of an instruction $t_{instruction\_cycle}$ is given by the following formula with c the number of periods necessary for its execution:

$$t_{clock\_cycle} = c \times t_{machine\_cycle} \tag{2.3}$$

It should be noted that the execution time of an instruction is preferably indicated in the datasheet (*cf.* Chapter 6) of the microprocessor in number of cycles c to be independent of the frequency of the clock. The parameter c will depend on the architecture, the operation itself and the addressing mode. For the RISC (Reduced Instruction Set Computer) architecture, this is constant, whereas this is not the case in a CISC (Complex Instruction Set Computer) architecture like x86. This information is then specified for each instruction. Figure 2.11 shows the breakdown of the instruction cycle into machine cycles for iconic MPUs.

$$t_{instruction\_execution} = t_{instruction\_search} + t_{instruction\_decoding}$$
$$+ t_{operand(s)\_search} + t_{effective\_execution} \tag{2.4}$$

Remember that access (to the memory) to execute an instruction is measured in bus cycles (*cf.* § V2-1.5) which, itself, is expressed in clock cycle or in machine cycle.

To conclude, here are the different times related to accessing information in memory. We must distinguish access to the instruction code from that linked to the operands.

$$t_{total\_memory\_access} = (t_{instruction\_fetch\_memory\_access} + t_{operand\_fetch\_memory\_access}) \times \frac{seconds}{period}$$

$$t_{instruction\_fetch\_memory\_access} = nb\_instruction\_fetch \times \frac{bus\_cycles}{instruction\_fetch} \times \frac{periods}{bus\_cycle}$$

$$t_{operand\_fetch\_memory\_access} = nb\_operands \times \frac{bus\_cycles}{operand\_fetch} \times \frac{periods}{bus\_cycle}$$

The performance of an MPU (*cf.* § V4-3.1) depends to a large extent on the timing frequency. This aspect will be explained in § V4-3.4.1.

2.4.2. *Exchange protocol*

The processor, to communicate with the memory, must send an address and the type of access (read or write). If it is a write, it also sends the data. In the case of a read, it will read the data at a specific time. Figure 2.18 illustrates this point. Note that if there is only one slave component, an address decoder is redundant. But in this case, the CS (or CE) selection input of the component must be permanently activated, which permanently results in maximum current consumption.

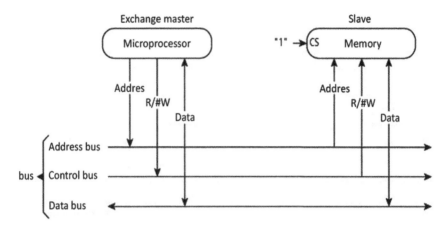

Figure 2.18. *Basic relationship between microprocessor and memory (I/O controllers not shown)*

To illustrate the protocol, the timing diagrams in Figure 2.19 detail the evolution of the signals as a function of time. As with the electrical aspect, the designer must make the protocols compatible. This can be done using external logic which will adapt the signals of the slave components to those of the master and vice versa. The cycle begins on the falling edge of the clock (time marker 1). The address becomes valid (i.e. usable) at time marker 2. The rising edge of the clock (time marker 3) allows temporal quantification of the maximum presentation time of the data to be written. The data read will be valid after an access time (time marker 5). The falling edge of the clock marks the end of a cycle with either the reading of the data by the master or its writing in the slave. These timing diagrams are to be matched in time with those of read and write access of a slave component such as a SRAM (Static RAM) and which are explained in § 4.2 of Darche (2012). The other types of transfer are read–modify–write (RMW) at the same address (an example is that of the MC68000, *cf.* § V4-2.6.1 on the atomic instructions for bit manipulation of microcontroller I/O ports (or MCU for MicroController Unit) 8051) and normal burst modes, such as the MC68030, or pipelined burst operated by the Pentium. They mainly concern memory, and they were detailed in Darche (2012).

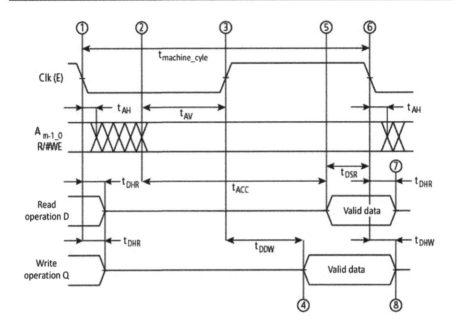

Figure 2.19. *Chronograms of a memory access cycle by the MC6802 microprocessor*

In the case of a slower component, it may be necessary to slow down the microprocessor. Figure 2.20 shows a reading and then a writing followed by a reading whose cycle has been extended for the MC68000 microprocessor from Motorola. For the latter case, WS (Wait State) cycles are inserted under the command of the #DTACK signal, the state of which is sampled on the falling edge of the state[6] S4 of this second reading (dotted arrows in the figure). This functionality therefore makes it possible to synchronize slower components slower than the master. Many MPUs have proposed it, such as the Z80 from Zilog or the Transputer (*cf.* § 5.5) from INMOS.

NOTE.– Why are signals often active at the low state (associated naming convention #<signal_name>)? It is for a question of stability at the voltage level. Indeed, it must be considered that the signal is active for a time shorter than that when the signal is not. The low state corresponds most of the time to 0 volts; it is also the return to ground. This line is often "polluted" electrically (i.e. parasitic). At rest, the signal is less disturbed, since at a stable level, it is therefore less likely to trigger nuisance trips. Furthermore, if the gate outputs are of the open collector or drain type

---

6 Here called "state" of a duration of a state of a clock period. An internal cycle lasts two clock periods.

(*cf.* § 2.3.2 and 2.4.2 of Darche (2004)) with pull-up resistor, then the current consumption is less.

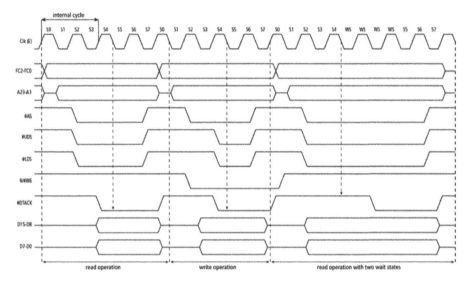

Figure 2.20. *Chronograms of a reading with and without wait states and a writing of an MC68000*

2.4.3. *Asynchronism*

Synchronism has many faults. The clock is always running and the logic circuits clocked by it therefore also operate continuously. This implies a permanent current consumption proportional to the operating frequency (*cf.* § 6.1.2). Consumption peaks appear with each change of state, introducing a power supply noise. The longest path in the combinatorial circuit determines the minimum period of the clock. Also, from a design point of view, it is necessary to predict the worst-case time based on other electrical, thermal and other characteristics, which has a detrimental effect. Furthermore, the propagation time of this signal becomes too long compared to the current operating frequency.

The basic idea of asynchronism is to design independent logical units (Clark 1967) and therefore to suppress the global clock which paces the entire system. The management signals necessary for communication between these units are presented in Volume 2 (*cf.* § V2-1.3). The aforementioned problems related to the clock such as the propagation delay and the skew between signals (temporal characteristics presented respectively in § 1.3 and 3.5.3 of Darche (2004)) no longer exist. The circuit consumes current only during its operation (i.e. a calculation), ideal for low-consumption systems such as mobile devices. Heterogeneous models in terms of time characteristics can be interconnected.

Asynchronism was already implemented in precursor computers like the ILLIAC and the Atlas. The pipeline is a subset that can exploit the benefits of asynchronism as studied (Sutherland 1989) under the term "micropipeline". A performance gain is obtained in these circuits (Franklin and Pan 1993). The first asynchronous MPU is that of Martin *et al.* (1989). Another pioneering example is the AMULET family (1 to 3) running the RISC®-inspired Arm® instruction set. This field is beyond the scope of this volume; for more information, see Van Berkel *et al.* (1999) and Sutherland and Ebergen (2002), which present an introduction to this field.

2.5. Conclusion

This chapter has detailed the interface of the microprocessor which is carried out first of all by the various communication buses as well as the other control and status signals. It ended with the time aspects mainly related to the clock.

Internal Constitution

A central unit or its integrated version, the MPU (MicroProcessor Unit), is made up of several functional units, of which the two main ones (Figure 3.1) are the Integer Unit (IU), called more precisely Arithmetic and Logic Unit (ALU), and the Control Unit (CU), which controls it, and a set of storage elements, registers (register array or file), participating in their operation. These constituent elements will now be detailed.

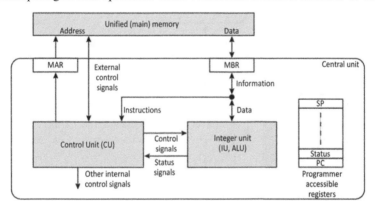

Figure 3.1. *Internal functional structure of a central unit*

3.1. Registers

We studied the notion of register in Chapter 3 of Darche (2002) devoted to sequential logic illustrated below with their use in Input–Output (I/O) controllers[1]

---

1 There are indeed "mapped" registers (i.e. projected) in memory (memory-mapped register) in I/O or bus controllers. They are called CSR (Control and Status Register, *cf.* § 2.1.1.1). In general, they have a different address space from that of data (CSR and data address spaces).

(*cf.* Chapter 3 of Darche (2003)). This section, after a definition, presents the various registers encountered. It ends with their involvement in the execution of instructions.

3.1.1. *Definition*

A register is made up of a set of n Flip-Flops or FF (in the case of logic in static version) whose function is, for each of them, to store a bit. The parallel register is the memory element of the microprocessor. This is called an n-bit register, for example, an 8-bit register. It is a fast memory with a capacity of a word in an format n. The qualifier "fast" means that the register operates at the speed of the component that integrates it so as not to slow it down by searching for information in the main memory or, to a lesser extent, in the cache memory. In a microprocessor, thanks to its latency being compatible with the functioning of the latter, it is naturally at the top of the hierarchy of memories (*cf.* Figure V1-2.5 and § 1.2 of Darche (2012)). If we restore the microprocessor registers in a computer (Figure 3.2), it is possible to add to its definition that it is a short-term memory close to the component that uses it (local or localized memory) as opposed to other subsets or components of the hierarchy.

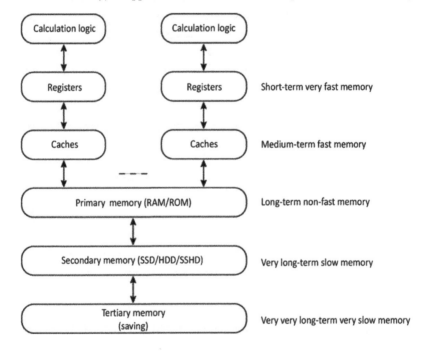

Figure 3.2. *Positioning of the registers of a microprocessor in the memory hierarchy*

This definition is to be qualified because, in a marginal way, the registers can be stored in main memory (Random Access Memory (RAM)-based register). This was the case with the TMS 9900, 16-bit microprocessor from the company Texas Instruments (*cf.* § 4.5). A WP (Workspace Pointer) was used to address its six registers. To access these, their number was added to the content of this pointer. The interest lays in a very rapid change of context since it was enough to change the value of the WP. During a subroutine call, the old values of the three registers accessible to the programmer (i.e. PC (Program Counter), WP and ST, *cf.* § 3.1) were stored in the last three locations of the workspace so that they could be returned to the caller. This avoided the use of a time-consuming stack when switching context (*cf.* § V4-4.2.2). Another interesting example is the PDP-10 from Digital Equipment Corporation (DEC), which had its 16 general-purpose registers AC in the address space of the main memory (addresses ranging from 0 to 15). The interest lays in the fact that they could be implemented, either in the same main memory technology or with faster components, the criterion of choice being economical.

Following the same line of thought, a register can be projected in memory. Called MMR for Memory-Mapped Register, it offers the programmer a homogeneous designation of memory locations that then uses a pointer to access its content. The register is however still physically in the MPU. The digital signal processors (DSP, *cf.* § 5.2) of TI's C5000 family is an example. The first 96 places on page 0 are reserved for this use. This functionality should not be confused with the implementation of the registers in primary memory of certain processors and microprocessors (see above).

Enumerating and characterizing the registers of a processor is one of the important points of the specification of the ISA (Instruction Set Architecture, *cf.* § V1-3.5). A register is used for internal storage of information of a diverse nature, numerical, whole or not, or alphanumeric. Its content can be specialized (SPR for Special-Purpose Register or SFR for Special Function Register). The address A[7:0] and data D[7:0] registers of the MPU MC68000 or the classic status registers and Stack Pointer (SP) are examples. Their name may not be explicit like the ordinal counter (i.e. PC). In micro-architecture, we have the classic MDR or MBR (Memory Data or Buffer Register) and MAR (Memory Address Register) registers, which are responsible for the processor interface with the external buses. Specializing one or more registers is penalizing for programming and compilation. The solution was to trivialize the content with the General-Purpose Register (GPR), by contrast, the other registers being qualified as Special (Purpose) Registers (SPR). The concept of general-purpose registers appeared with the PEGASUS (Elliott *et al.* 1956) of the company Ferranti Ltd (Siewiorek *et al.* 1982), and we find this idea with the CDP1802 (COSMAC for Complementary Symmetry Monolithic Array Computer) and the CP1600 (*cf.* respectively § 4.3 and 4.5). To a lesser extent, another example is registers A to D of the MPU 8086 from Intel. GPR and SPR are therefore registry classes. Thus, due to their access, a register is said to be architectured (architected register or architected resource) when it is accessible (i.e. usable) to the programmer as opposed to an implemented register, which is accessed only by the internal machine and therefore invisible to the programmer. This second category contains the state of the machine. Examples are the register scoreboard, the ReOrder Buffer (ROB), the inter-stage pipeline latch and the history buffer for branches and more.

The most common registers are the accumulator (AC), auxiliary or standardized registers; the program counter (PC), the Instruction Register (IR), the status register, the index register and the stack pointer (SP). The accumulator differs from a trivialized register by the fact that it is generally used implicitly in arithmetic calculations. The origin of its name indicates that it cumulated the calculation results (*cf.* § V1-3.2.2.1). We can also cite MQ (Multiplier-Quotient) register of the original von Neumann machine (*cf.* § V1-3.2.2.3). Certain registers are more particularly, or even exclusively, used by one or other of the functional units.

The first central units had only one accumulator. Subsequently, the number of registers increased. In the extended accumulator, or SPR or dedicated architecture, the accumulator is no longer the only register. On the contrary, it has several registers with reserved or restricted uses. The 8086 is an example of this architecture. The constraint for these two architectures is that an operand must reside in main memory. Other MPUs, on the other hand, do not specialize in use like the Arm® and MIPS families. The architecture is named general-purpose register architecture. You always have to qualify. A register can be dedicated (i.e. to a function) or specialized, not dedicated or partially. If we take the Arm® family with 16 Ri registers, (i ∈ [0, 15]). R15 is dedicated because it is PC (Program Counter). R14 is semi-dedicated to saving the return address when calling a subroutine (other name: link register). The rest are free to use. Despite this, these two registers can be used by the programmer. It is clear that the trivialization of PC and SP in a general-purpose register offers progress as new addressing possibilities and contributes to the "power" of the MPU.

A register can be accessed in write and/or read. Some registers are accessible to the programmer[2] (programmer-accessible or user-accessible register), others not, others indirectly (Table 3.1). For the latter, it is necessary to carry out various operations to access it, for example, by a stacking on the stack, by specialized instruction as in the case of MCS6502 or during a saving of context during a call to a subroutine (*cf.* § V4-4.2), then a modification of its content, to finish with a destacking, which restores the register with the modified value. As these are registers internal to the CPU (Central Processing Unit), they are accessible in another way rather than with an address. In assembly language, they are accessible by their name. They can also be accessed implicitly (*cf.* § V4-1.2.4.6). The registers in an I/O

2 We also say "visible to the programmer".

controller are a counter-example because they have a direct or indirect address (i.e. two-step access), which can belong to their own address space (*cf.* § 2.1.1.1).

Registers	Accessibility by the programmer
Accumulator	Direct
Auxiliary registers	Direct
Program counter	Indirect by software sequence
Instruction register	Not available
Status register	Indirect
Index register	Direct
Stack pointer	Direct

Table 3.1. *Accessibility of the main registers of a microprocessor*

The format of a register can be variable depending on the type of data. An example is the DSP TMS320C31 extended precision register, which can receive a 32-bit natural or relative integer or a 40-bit floating-point number (mantissa and exponent). When an integer is received, the bits b[39:32] remain unchanged and will not be modified in the event of shift operations. Some registers such as accumulators and trivialized registers can be concatenated like for the MC6809, the Z80 or, more recently, the Intel family processors. This makes it possible to double the data processing format and thus to perform arithmetic operations such as multiplication which requires a format double that of the two operands (Figure 3.3).

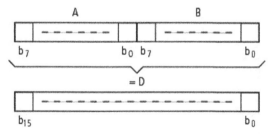

Figure 3.3. *Concatenation of the two accumulators of the MC6809*

Another example is the 8086 with its data registers A to D in 16-bit format, which can be broken down into two registers in byte format. Their name is suffixed by the letter l (for low) for the lower part, h (for high) for the upper part and x for the 16-bit version. For reasons of ascending compatibility (*cf.* § V4-3.3.3), in the IA[3]-32 architecture, the format of the general registers of the 8086 was then extended to 32 bits by prefixing with the letter e (for extended) the name of the register already associated with the suffix x. There are thus the general registers, EAX, EBX, ECX, EDX, EBP, ESP, EDI and ESI, the lower part (16-bit format) broken down into two bytes is accessible in assembly language by removing the prefix "E" and using the suffix h or l. The length of the instructions remains variable. In the same way, the company Intel then extended the format to 64 bits with the prefix r meaning "64-bit extension register". We will thus have the registers RAX, RBX, RCX, RDX, RBP, RSP, RDI and RSI (Figure 3.4). In terms of encoding, the prefix allows in 64-bit mode to extend the format of the registers. It is automatically added by the assembler to maintain backward compatibility (*cf.* § V4-3.3). Despite a 64-bit architecture format, the operand size is 32 bits by default. If a calculation is performed on 32 bits, then the result is stored in a 64-bit register with stuffing bits at 0. If the format is 16 or 8 bits, then the bits above the format remain unchanged.

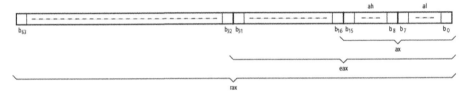

Figure 3.4. *Designation of register A of x86 family microprocessors depending on the format*

Let us now detail each type of register cited.

3.1.2. *Accumulators and auxiliary registers*

Historically, the primary function of the accumulator, from which its name is derived, has been the algebraic addition (Bartee and Chapman 1965). It could also calculate other arithmetic functions, such as multiplication and division, or logical functions (Quatse and Keir 1967). Today, the accumulator is a special register which implicitly receives the result of an operation. It can also be used by the programmer. Several accumulators can coexist as in the PACE 4 microprocessor (Fox and Reyling 1975; Weissberger 1975). An example is the rA register, the accumulator of Donald Knuth's hypothetical MIX computer (Knuth 1968).

---

3 For Intel Architecture.

Auxiliary or generalized registers can be implemented to allow data to be stored in order to increase execution speed. Indeed, access to a register is always faster than access to a main memory. The RISC (Reduced Instruction Set Computer, this will be covered in a future book by the author on microprocessors), MIPS (Microprocessor without Interlocked Pipeline Stages), DLX (DeLuXe, Sailer and Kaeli 1996) and Arm® microprocessors, for example, designate these registers with the letter r indicated (r0, r1, etc.). Some have a constant value 0, 1 or -1. The zero register r0 of the aforementioned companies or of the MPU 88100 of the company Motorola is an example. It contains the null value in a wired way. It is only accessible for reading but can be used as a trash register if a result is not useful. Zero is the reference test value (*cf.* § V4-2.4.1), and this avoids memory access to fetch it. There are also Floating-Point Registers (FPR) in the unit of the same name.

3.1.3. *Program counter*

The program counter (PC), also called ILR (Instruction-Location Register) and rarely called the ordinal counter, contains the address of the next instruction which will be executed by the microprocessor, an exception being the SC/MP (*cf.* § 4.3). The other name that can be encountered is Instruction Pointer (IP) at Intel. Due to its function, this register is undoubtedly one of the most important for the processor. The address it contains is presented on the address bus during the fetch cycle. The content of this register is updated during the decoding cycle to anticipate the execution of the next one because the value of the PC (Program Counter) incrementation is a function of the size (i.e. its number of bytes) of the instruction in running. Thus, n being the number of bytes of the instruction being executed:

$$PC \leftarrow PC + 1 \text{ in RTL}^4 \Rightarrow PC = PC + n$$

In the event of a break in the execution sequence (i.e. jump), the jump address must take this fact into account. It is a control register. This address, instead of occupying a whole register, could be integrated into another. Thus, bits b[63:40] of the PSW (Program Status Word) of the IBM System/360 and /370 formed the PC (Program Counter). Normally, this register is not accessible directly by designation in a program, but indirectly by an index, for example, by stacking on the stack then accessing. Some MPUs use a general-purpose register (GPR) for this function. For the Arm® family, for example, in the Cortex-M and ARMv7 series, this is the r15 register. This definition is to be nuanced with advanced architectures of the pipelined type and out-of-order execution. We talk about this in a future book on microprocessors.

---

4 This will be covered in a future book by the author on microprocessors.

3.1.4. *Instruction register*

During the fetch cycle, the CPU will search the main memory for the code of the instruction to be executed and store it in the instruction register (IR) so that it can be decoded (*cf.* § 3.4.3.2). The latter receives these codes from the main memory or better from the cache memory, directly or via an instruction queue or buffer. It is also called the Current Instruction Register (CIR).

3.1.5. *Status and control register*

This register is made up of (binary) status indicators (condition codes) or status flags, hence the synonym names of indicator flags or Status flags Register (SR[5]). These provide information on the current state of the processor. They play a fundamental role because it is thanks to them, for example, that it is possible to carry out a conditional branch (*cf.* § V4-2.4.1) in the sequential execution of instructions by the processor (condition control flow). It is for this reason that it is also called Condition Code Register (CCR), program status word (PSW[6] or program status byte depending on the format), status register of the program (PSR for Program Status word Register), for example, for the SPARC architecture (Scalable Processor ARChitecture) or current program status register (CPSR) of the Arm® family. Note that some MPUs like Motorola's 88100 (Alsup 1990) use any general-purpose register as their status register. This eliminates certain operational hazards of pipelines when there are dependencies on the result of a branch condition. This aspect is developed in a future book by the author on microprocessors, which deals with the pipeline. The condition codes are the result of the encoding of the different conditions, hence the name. A format n of a condition field makes it possible to obtain 2^n possible cases of condition. If n is 1 then it is a binary indicator. We must distinguish three types of flags, status or result, control and system type. There are result flags for the different representations of numbers which can be combined in a single register or separated.

3.1.5.1. *Flags for whole numbers*

After execution of certain instructions, the status flags inform the processor and, consequently, the programmer, about the status of the execution result and, in particular, about its validity. We can first distinguish the integer condition codes. Examples of status are the indicators of zero (ZF for Zero (status) Flag), of sign (SF for Sign (status) Flag), also called NF (Negative Flag), and of logical parity

---

5 ST for TMS 9900 from Texas Instruments.

6 Origin is IBM System/360 architecture.

(PF for Parity (status) Flag). The carry (CF or CY[7] for Carry (status) Flag) and half-carry (H[8]) flag, AF or AC for auxiliary carry (status) flag[9] or DC for digit carry flag[10] indicators also retained intermediate (intermediate carry flag) and, finally, arithmetic overflow (OF for Overflow (status) Flag or VF for oVerflow (status) Flag), positive or negative, provide information on the correctness of a result of an arithmetic calculation on natural or relative integers according to the flag. The restraint is used by the addition in natural binary (NB(C) for Natural Binary (Code)) to indicate a format overflow as well as by the whole subtraction. It then plays the role of a borrow (status) flag. The half-carry flag is useful for calculations in Binary Coded Decimal (BCD, *cf.* § II.1.2 of Darche (2000)). The integer overflow only makes sense in the Two's Complement representation, also called complement on 2^n representation (i.e. a signed integer representation therefore for relative integer, *cf.* § II.2.5 of Darche (2000)), but some manufacturers such as (AMD 1987) use the term unsigned overflow for restraint as opposed to "classic" overflow, which will be called "signed". Thanks to them, it is possible to perform a conditional jump. Indeed, any condition is reduced to a subtraction with positioning of the binary indicators (*cf.* § V4-2.4.1).

Let us cite some specific examples of implementation. The extension bit (eXtend bit) X of the MC68000 plays the role of the carry bit during a multi-precision addition or subtraction (`addx` and `subx` instructions). The Q flag of ISA ARMv5 and higher makes it possible to detect an arithmetic overflow and/or saturation. Note that this is a sticky bit which, once set to 1, can only go back to its inactive state by executing the `msr` specialized instruction. The displacement-type instructions (`movx`, `mnegx` and `mcom`) of the VAX processor (Virtual Addressed eXtended) from the company Digital Equipment Corporation (DEC) update flags according to the value moved, while certain MPUs like those of the architecture x86 do not position them during a transfer (*cf.* § V4-2.2.1).

As the implementations are heterogeneous, some components have only a subset of the indicators presented. For example, the ICC (Integer Condition Codes) and XCC (eXtended Condition Codes for 64-bit format) fields of the SPARC architecture, which only have NZVC flags. Certain indicators can probably be grouped together to gain a bit. An example is the P/V indicator of the Z80, which groups the P and V flags. It indicates the logical parity when executing logical instructions and the overflow when executing arithmetic instructions, the distinction

---

7 MPU 8080A from Intel.

8 The origin is the MC6800 microprocessor from Motorola, later used by the Z80 from Zilog.

9 The origin is the microprocessor 8080 from Intel.

10 The origin is the PIC architecture of General Instrument then Microchip Technology Inc.

according to the instruction executed. A special feature to note of the AVR microcontrollers from the company Atmel which distinguishes the sign bit N, recopy of the highest position bit and useful in an interpretation of the data in sign and module of the bit S (Sign) which indicates the polarity of a result in complement on 2^n representation (*cf.* exercise E3.4). A theoretical machine must have flags. An example is that of the rA register (Knuth 1999; Anlauff *et al.* 2002) of the MMIX architecture (Knuth 2004; Ruckert 2015). Figure 3.5 shows the status register of four representative microprocessors of the second generation of microprocessors. The original acronyms have been retained. The B (Break) flag indicates that a software interrupt is being executed. A copy of the status register is stacked with this flag set to "1". This makes it possible to distinguish an interrupt routine from a classic routine (i.e. equivalent to a function or a procedure, *cf.* § V4-4.2).

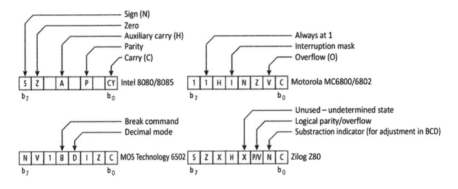

Figure 3.5. *Four MPU indicator registers representative of the 8-bit generation*

It is possible to consider the flags as results derived from a calculation and its result. They can thus be divided into two groups, implicit and explicit. A, C and V (Flag), derived from the operation executed, belong to the first group and the flags Z, P, N and S, derived from the result, to the second. Hennessy *et al.* (1982a) identifies four uses of status flags which are the conditional break in the control flow, the evaluation of a boolean expression, multi-precision[11] arithmetic and the detection of overflow.

3.1.5.2. *Flags for numbers in the decimal representation*

The D flag (decimal flag) of the MCS6502 allows you to configure the ALU so that it performs calculations in decimal mode with numbers coded in BCD (*cf.* § V4-2.1), a principle which has been patented (Peddle *et al.* 1976). This avoids

---

11 It allows manipulating arbitrary format numbers.

the use of an adjustment instruction (*cf.* § V4-2.3.1) and, possibly, programming errors.

3.1.5.3. *Flags for fixed-point numbers*

The PowerPC microprocessor has four flags, which are Less_Than (LT), Greater_Than (GT), EQual (EQ) and Summary Overflow (SO). The first two indicate whether the result of a fixed-point arithmetic calculation is negative or positive respectively or whether the first source operand is respectively lower or higher in the fixed-point and floating-point representations. The EQ flag indicates an equality or a zero result. The last is the copy of the overflow flag from the XER (fiXed-point Exception Register) for fixed-point calculations.

3.1.5.4. *Flags for floating-point numbers*

The calculations in the floating-point representation (FPR, *cf.* § II.4.2 of Darche (2000)) use its own condition codes (floating-point condition codes). They are called ELGU (Equal, Less, Greater and Unordered), for example, for SPARC and stored in the floating-point status register (FSR). Figure 3.6 presents the status word of the specialized status register of mathematical coprocessors or FPUs (Floating-Point Unit, *cf.* § 5.4) of the Intel x87 family (format n = 16 bits). In ascending order of bit position, the first six flags are exception flags. They respectively signal an invalid arithmetic operation (IE for Invalid operation Exception), a denormalized operand (DE for Denormalized operand Exception), a division by zero (ZE for divide-by-Zero or Zero divide Exception), an overflow exception (OE for numerical Overflow Exception) or underflow exception (UE for numerical Underflow Exception) or an inaccurate result (PE for inexact-result or Precision Exception). Bit 6 is the stack error flag (SF for Stack Fault) that indicates a stack overflow or underflow thanks to bit C1, which should not be confused with the classic SF flag of the status register of the ALU. SF is a sticky bit, which means that it can only be reset by an instruction. The following indicator (ES for Error Summary status) summarizes the previous exceptions, but if the exception concerned is hidden in the control register, then ES does not go to 1 and the processing routine (exception handler) is not invoked. The condition codes Ci (Condition Code i, i ∈ [3: 0]) are the result of a comparison or a floating-point arithmetic operation. The three bits forming the TOP field for Top-of-Stack Pointer specifies the number of the register, which is the top of the stack (*cf.* § V4-4.1). The last (B) is a unit occupancy indicator (Busy FPU).

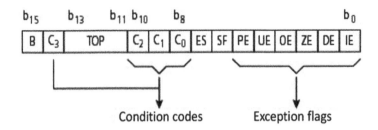

Figure 3.6. *X87 family floating-point computing unit status register*

The management of the integrated FPU in modern MPUs is complex. A representative example is the MIPS64® architecture (MIPS 2005) where the group of flags E (unimplemented operation), V, Z and O are instantiated three times[12] with different functions for the same designation for arithmetic operations (cause field), the authorization of exceptions (enabled field) linked to the origin and the exception indication (flags field) reset only by software. A final example is the exception control flags on overflow in decimal (decimal overflow trap enable), integer (integer overflow trap enable) and floating (floating underflow trap enable) representations.

3.1.5.5. *Condition codes*

The term "condition codes" originates from mainframe computers. It is a binary word that encodes a logical condition as shown in Table 3.2. If the code has a single bit format, then it is a binary indicator as it was for the first microprocessors.

3.1.5.6. *Control and system flags*

Originally, the flags were grouped in a dedicated register called condition register (CR) or, rarely, "indicator register" (IR). The role of this registry has evolved. It no longer provides information only on the status of a result. It can, by setting a bit, modify the behavior of an instruction such as branch or control the operation of the processor. This is called a control flag. It is positioned by the programmer according to the rights (*cf.* § V4-3.2.2). An example for the microprocessor x86 is the direction indicator (DF for Direction Flag). It is used to force the direction of transfer of a character string (i.e. respected or reverse order) from one memory area to another.

---

12 Except for flag E.

Opcode condition codes [31:28]				Correspondences (mnemonic extension)
0	0	0	0	Equal (EQ)
0	0	0	1	Not Equal (NE)
0	0	1	0	Carry Set (CS/HS)
0	0	1	1	Carry Clear (CC/LO)
0	1	0	0	MI (Minus/negative)
0	1	0	1	PL (Plus/positive or zero)
0	1	1	0	VS (Overflow)
0	1	1	1	VC (No overflow)
1	0	0	0	HI (Unsigned HIgher)
1	0	0	1	LS (Unsigned Lower or Same)
1	0	1	0	GE (Signed Greater than or Equal)
1	0	1	1	LT (Signed Less Than)
1	1	0	0	GT (Signed Greater Than)
1	1	0	1	LE (Signed Less than or Equal)
1	1	1	0	AL (ALways (unconditional))
1	1	1	1	Specific behavior

Table 3.2. *Condition codes and their meaning in ARM architecture*

The system flags allow you to implement a modern operating system. This sub-family makes it possible to control the general functioning of the microprocessor. At Intel, the two historical indicators are the interrupt mask (IF for Interrupt enable Flag) and the flag for step-by-step mode (TF for Trap Flag). The IF flag is used to authorize the consideration of a hardware[13] interrupt request such as IRQ (Interrupt Request). Positioned at 1, the TF flag allows an exception to be thrown at the end of each instruction execution to launch a debugger. Today, there are eight, I/O Privilege Level (IOPL), Nested Task flag (NT), Resume Flag (RF), Virtual-8086 Mode (VM), Alignment Check (AC), Virtual Interrupt Flag (VIF), Virtual Interrupt Pending flag

---

13 It should be noted that the PDP-11 had three bits setting the current priority interrupt bit level of the processor (priority interrupt bit) authorizing or not an external controller to interrupt it. Thus, setting the priority level to 7 prohibits any interruption.

(VIP) and IDentification flag (ID). The IOPL flag is used to find out the I/O privilege level of the current task. It also makes it possible to control the modification of the IF flag in virtual mode 8086. The NT indicator makes it possible to control the chaining of the tasks called by interruption, by exception or by a `call` instruction. Set to 1, it indicates to the current task that it has been called. It is initialized on execution of an `iret` instruction. RF (Resume Flag) controls the processor response to a breakpoint by temporarily disabling the debug exception. The VM flag allows passing from the protected mode to the virtual mode 8086. The AC (Alignment Check) indicator makes it possible to set up the control of the alignment of the memory words (*cf.* § V1-1.2 and § 2.6.1 of Darche (2012)) by generating an exception if a reference points to an unaligned operand. VIF contains a virtualized image of the IF flag. It is associated with the VIP flag, which indicates that an interruption is in progress. ID if a processor can change its state indicates that it supports the `cpuid` instruction (*cf.* § V4-2.5.5) allowing others to identify the type of processor. Figure 3.7 shows their position in the register. The unassigned bits have a state, either indeterminate (case of 8086) or determined in this case zero.

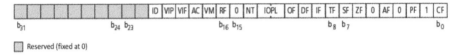

Reserved (fixed at 0)

Figure 3.7. *The IA-32 family EFLAGS register*

IT (InTerruption) management is generally global, but some MPUs have proposed individual masking. An example is the PACE 16-bit MPU for processing and control element (Fox and Reyling 1975; Weissberger 1975) from National Semiconductor (NS) with a global authorization flag IEN (master Interrupt ENable) and individual flags IE_i (individual Interrupt Enable, $i \in [1, 5]$). It should be noted that it had four general-purpose control flags F_i.

3.1.5.7. *Updating flags*

The flags, if they must be positioned, are at the end of the execution of an instruction (*cf.* § on the side effects below), but not all of them do so. It will depend on the microprocessor. For example, an addition with an x86 family MPU will update these while the `mov` instruction will not. An indicator can have a temporary state, until the next instruction likely to modify it by the result. This is the case with status flags. This can be an obstacle to optimizing the code generated in assembly language by the compiler. It is for this reason that in the control structures, the instruction updating the flags (i.e. arithmetic or classical logical or test/comparison instructions) is "stuck" to the conditional jump instructions. Or, if there is an instruction block (i.e. a series of contiguous instructions) in between, these interleaved instructions should not change the flags. However, it is also an advantage because the condition codes facilitate the implementation of multiple branches (*cf.* § V4-2.4.1).

The flag can also have a permanent state. This is the case for control or system flags. They then make it possible to modify the behavior of certain instructions, for example, when processing character string or the processor for, for example, execution in step-by-step mode or the masking of interrupts. Their state will be modified by direct action on the indicator by specialized instruction such as cli and sti, which respectively inhibits or authorizes material interrupts (maskable). For the indirect way, you have to stack the status register, either with a specialized instruction like pushf (x86) or during a subroutine call, then perform on the stack the manipulation of bit(s) by masking and, finally, restore the registry by unstacking the value either by instruction (popf) or by performing a subroutine return. If we observe a documentation (*cf.* Appendix 1), for each instruction, the state of the flag register is given. By generalizing to the state of a bit, the conventions for its state will be as follows: "0" or "1", sometimes S for Set, for forcing to a logical state, "-" for an unchanged state (i.e. not affected by the instruction), "?" for an unknown or undetermined state after execution and """" or "*" for a modification after execution. Sometimes there is just the list of indicators that are affected and undefined (*cf.* Appendix 2).

During a branch (call to a subroutine or to an interrupt handler), the content of the CCR can be saved on the stack (*cf.* § V4-4.1). This is what is called the execution context (*cf.* § V4-4.2.2). Upon return to the caller, the caller can be restored so that the execution of the subroutine is "transparent" to the caller, that is, as if it had not taken place.

3.1.6. *Index register*

The index register (IR) was introduced to facilitate the programming of data structure access. An example is an access to a data in an array. For this, it is necessary to use advanced addressing modes such as indexing, the index register used to develop the indexed address. The effective address is obtained by adding its content with the address of an operand (*cf.* indexed and based addressing modes, *cf.* § V4-1.2.3.4). There may be an automatic increment and decrement option. This register appeared under the name of B-line the first time with the Mark I of the University of Manchester in 1949 (Lavington 1980; Smith 1989) then, subsequently, under the name of B-register (*cf.* example with the DATATRON model 204 computer (Burroughs 1956)). It is also called a "modifier register". 'We find for example this type of register under the names BX, BP, DI and SI for, respectively Base Pointer, Destination and Source Index, in x86 architecture (cf. § V4-1.2.3.4 and 1.2.4.1).'.

3.1.7. *Indirection register*

This register allows indirect addressing (*cf.* § V4-1.2.3.3). It contains an address allowing access to a memory location. It is used to implement the notion of pointer.

3.1.8. *Stack pointer register*

Its acronym is SP for stack pointer. During a diversion among others, it is necessary to save certain information, the most important of which is the return address to the caller. The stack pointer allows, as its name suggests, pointing to either the memory location where it is possible to store information, or the last location where a backup took place. If the processor has two operating modes, supervisor and user, there can be two separate pointers, the system and user stack pointers (*cf.* § V4-4.1). An example is the NS16000 from NS, which has a separate stack pointer depending on the execution mode. An IS/US (Interrupt Stack/User Stack) flag in the status register indicates which battery is being used. Another example is the MC6809, which has two stack pointers, the registers S for hardware stack pointer and U for user stack pointer. The former is used by the MPU during subroutine and interrupt handler calls. The latter is available for the programmer to manage the parameters. As with PC, SP can be a GPR. Let us quote r13 for the Arm® cortex-M family and R6 for the PDP-11 minicomputer. The use of this register will be detailed in Chapters V4-4 and V4-5.

3.1.9. *Special registers*

Depending on the implementations, there may be feature-specific registers. Let us cite the registers specific to virtual memory management (this will be covered in a future book by the author on memories) with the basic registers of the IBM System/360 and /370 computers or the segmentation registers (code, data, extra and stack) and descriptor table registers (GDTR – Global Descriptor Table Register, LDTR – Local Descriptor Table Register, IDTR – Interrupt Descriptor Table Register) of the x86 family of Intel. In the latter, registers are used to control the behavior of the processor (control registers CR0-4 and CR8 (64-bit generation only)), for its (self-) test (test registers TR7-6 (80386 and 80486) and TR5-3 (80486 only) and replaced in Pentium by Model-Specific Registers (MSR) and debugging (registers (DR3-0, 6 and 7). Task registers (TR) appeared with the 80386.

Another example is the refresh register (or counter) of the Z80 microprocessor useful for managing DRAM (Dynamic RAM), which generates an associated external signal. On the same theme, the AMC 80C186 includes a Refresh Control Unit (RCU) with two associated management registers. Also in memory management, there are the control register or MTRR (Memory Type Range Register) introduced from the Intel P6 family for memory and cache management. Cache memories require specialized registers such as the TLB (Translation Lookaside Buffer), which allows the most recent translations from the virtual address to the physical address to be stored in the MMU (Memory Management Unit, this will be covered in a future book by the author on memories) to speed up access to memory. That of the Am29000 is a cache memory of 64 entries.

Finally, let us cite the loop hardware management registers (*cf.* § V4-2.4.3) and the identification registers. These give information about the component. The identification initially concerned only a serial number (e.g. MicroController Unit architecture (MCU) PIC32), then it was extended to different hardware and software characteristics (*cf.* § V4-2.5.5). Intel x86, AMD and RISC-V architectures offer this comprehensive functionality.

3.1.10. *Synthesis*

Figures 3.8 and 3.9 show all the registers of four major 8-bit generation microprocessors. Their format is indicated in brackets. It is mainly distinguished by their number. The Z80 stood out for its backward compatibility (*cf.* § V4-3.3.3) with the 8080 from the company Intel preceding it in these registers as shown in Figure 3.8. Its data registers and that of the indicators were also duplicated to form an alternative register bank, which allowed a rapid change of context when processing an interrupt request (*cf.* Chapter V4-5) and avoided saving of these on the stack which was time-consuming. This idea was taken up with multi-threading (this will be covered in a future book by the author on microprocessors). Two other Z80 registers are not shown. These are the interrupt page address register I (interrupt page address or interrupt vector) in byte format and the memory refresh register R in 7-bit format (*cf.* previous section).

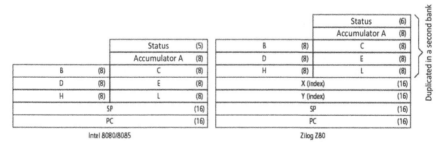

Figure 3.8. *Set of registers of two representative 8-bit generation microprocessors*

Figure 3.9 shows the backward compatibility of the MCS6502, which shows the registers of the MC6800.

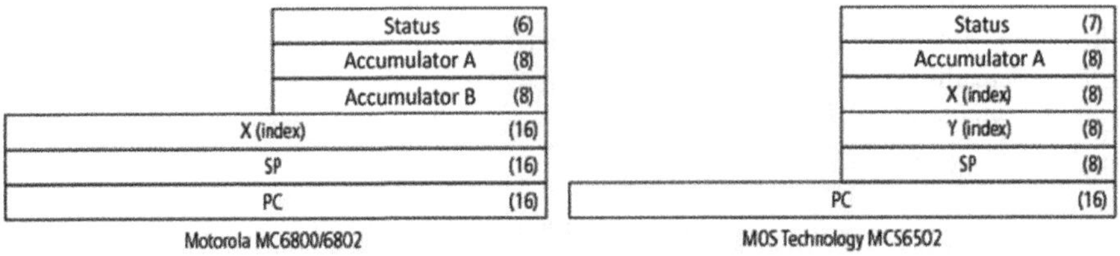

Status	(6)
Accumulator A	(8)
Accumulator B	(8)
X (index)	(16)
SP	(16)
PC	(16)

Motorola MC6800/6802

Status	(7)
Accumulator A	(8)
X (index)	(8)
Y (index)	(8)
SP	(8)
PC	(16)

MOS Technology MCS6502

Figure 3.9. *Set of registers of two representative microprocessors of the 8-bit generation (continuation and end)*

3.1.11. *Register structures*

The registers of an MPU are generally grouped in a structure. Three existing structures are the file, the bank and the windowing.

3.1.11.1. *Register file*

A Register File (RF) is a set of registers used to store operands. It is a memory with multiple access or port (multiport memory). The classic version is an array of registers with two read and one write ports connected to separate buses. The distributed register file version offered by Forsell (1996) has an external input and n outputs. This RF is generally presented in front of an ALU. It can also be used at the path level as suggested (Goosens 2003; Goossens and Defour 2005). Access to the register file is done simply by decoding the register number allowing access to a single register (Figure 3.10). The addressing described here is linear. Access can also be in the stack as described in § V4-4.1.

From an implementation point of view, an RF occupies almost as much space on the surface as an ALU. An example is the CDP1802 with a set of 16 registers (register array R) in 16-bit format. The zero page (*cf.* § V4-1.2.3.1 and V4-1.2.4.7) of the address space of an MPU can be seen as such an RF (Register File). The register file can be organized into banks (multiple-banked RF) as proposed (Cruz *et al.* 2000), the subdivision allowing the reduction of access time. The design of this subset is critical for performance in parallel environments (this will be covered in a future book by the author on microprocessors).

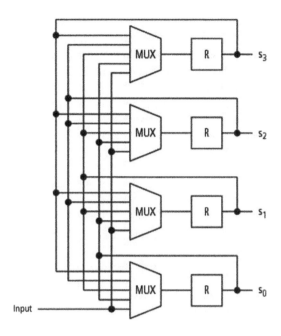

Figure 3.10. *Functional block diagram of a distributed register file (Forsell 1996)*

3.1.11.2. *Bank register*

The above structure should not be confused with banked registers. It is a question here of having several copies of a register or several registers. For example, the Am29000 has 16 banks of 16 registers with a Register Bank Protect (RBP) register where one of its 16 bits is used to control write or read access in user mode. These copies are useful in an environment with several execution modes (*cf.* § V4-3.2.2 for an example). This mechanism allows rapid context switching.

3.1.11.3. *Windowing of registers*

The windowing (of the file) of registers (register file windowing or multiple-window register file) (Huguet and Lang 1985) makes it easy and above all quick to pass the parameters between caller and called (Dannenberg 1979; Sites 1979; Lampson 1982). This is detailed in § V4-4.2.3. For window management, there are pointer registers (Window Pointer Register) and window masking registers. Window pointer registers contain the address of active registers. It allows you to change the mapping of registers by making a window active. Window masking registers contain one bit per window signaling all registers containing valid data. As shown in Figure 3.11, in the case of a SPARC MPU, the windowed registers function as a circular buffer. It should be noted that these windows overlap (overlapping register windows, *cf.* § V4-4.2.3). The register named CWP (Current Window Pointer) manages the current window, the register WIM (Window Invalid Mask) allowing invalidating a window. When this buffer is full and there is a backup request, there is then a windows overflow. In this case, a mechanism to save one or two windows to a spill memory is implemented. When the restoration takes place and therefore a return to a normal situation, we speak of a window underflow.

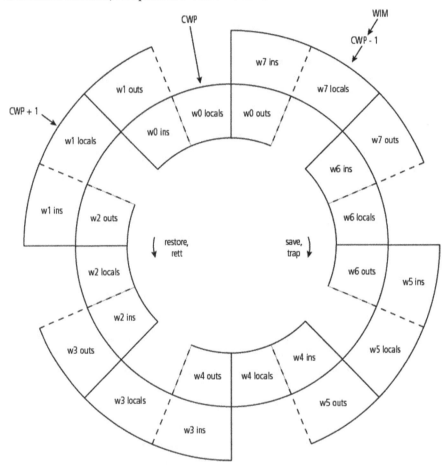

Figure 3.11. *SPARC family register window (Hall and Barry 1990; Catanzaro 1991)*

There are several forms of windowing (Figure 3.13) related to the size or the access method. The SPARC family microprocessors and the RISC II (Katevenis *et al*. 1983; Patterson 1984) have a fixed size. This has the disadvantage of not offering flexibility as to the number of parameters and local variables. The 29K family of microprocessors from AMD uses a variable size. To manage a variable size, it is necessary to manage a window start pointer implemented in the form of a register called SWP (Saved Window Pointer) in Figure 3.12. Each access to a register is the result of the addition of its value with the reference of the register to which we want to access, the calculation being done materially for a reason of time cost. This is to achieve an access relative to the window considered. A final variant is called shifting register windows (Russell and Shaw 1993). Operation is based on stack operation of the register bank. When there is an overflow, a backup of the registry is made in main memory.

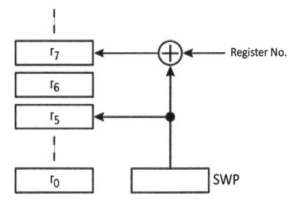

Figure 3.12. *Relative addressing of window registers*

Figure 3.13 summarizes the three solutions mentioned above.

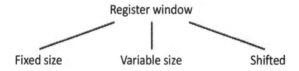

Figure 3.13. *Classification of register windows*

The disadvantage of windowing is a significant occupation of the surface of the chip (at the time). This windowing mechanism has been implemented in microprocessors, first at the research level with RISC I and II and then at the industrial level in the SPARC architecture. The IA-64 microprocessor is not a RISC (this will be covered in a future book by the author on microprocessors) from Intel who then offered it.

3.1.12. *Notions related to registers*

The use of registers leads to a phenomenon called "side effect", which is not wanted when calling a subroutine or when executing instructions in parallel. In addition, their number has a consequence on the format of the encoded instruction. All of these aspects are covered in this section.

3.1.12.1. *Side effect*

The execution of an instruction can be compared to that of a function with a possible side effect. A side effect is an unwanted effect following the execution of a calculable unit. An example for a function is the modification of an external entity as a global variable during its execution. The use of the status of a result by the following instructions (implicit passage of status) does not pose a problem in architecture with sequential execution, which is to say that of the first MPUs. In modern architectures which exploit execution parallelism as a pipeline (this will be covered in a future book by the author on microprocessors), the status indicators are seen as a side effect of the execution of an instruction and they are context-dependent. Another example is the Out-of-Order (OoO) execution with which it can be annoying that there is a dependency linked to the update at the end of the execution of an instruction that the next must take into account. A first solution is to insert costly waiting times (case of VAX). To eliminate or, at least, to limit this effect, several solutions exist. One solution is to duplicate the status register. The PowerPC (Diefendorf and Silha 1994) thus has eight condition[14] registers to avoid hazards. Another is to make the state transition explicit. The compiler or assembler then explicitly indicates that an instruction affects the flags by suffixing the instructions with cc. An example is that of the SPARC version 9 architecture, which allows you to update the ICC and XCC fields (*cf.* § 3.1.5.1 and § V4-2.4.2). Furthermore, the conditional branching is implemented in a single instruction and not two (comparison then conditional jump). MIPS, DEC Alpha or RISC-V does not have dedicated condition flags. Any register can have this function. The state also passes explicitly from one instruction to another. This type of approach consumes

---

14 Or, more precisely, eight sub-fields of four status flags to form a 32-bit register.

more instructions. All these ideas will be detailed in § V4-2.4.2 and especially in a future book by the author on microprocessors.

3.1.12.2. Context of execution

The context of execution consists of all the information linked to the execution of an instruction (*cf.* § V4-4.2.2). The MC6809 microprocessor has a flag named E, which indicates whether all the registers have been stored during a context saving.

3.1.12.3. Passing parameters

Registers are a way to pass the parameters of a subroutine. They can be organized in windows for an accelerated passage (*cf.* § 3.1.11.3 and § V4-4.2.3).

Privileged mode						
		Exception mode				
User	System	Supervisor	Abort	Undefined	Interruption	Fast interrupt
r0	r0	r0	r0	r0	r0	r0
r1	r1	r1	r1	r1	r1	r1
r2	r2	r2	r2	r2	r2	r2
r3	r3	r3	r3	r3	r3	r3
r4	r4	r4	r4	r4	r4	r4
r5	r5	r5	r5	r5	r5	r5
r6	r6	r6	r6	r6	r6	r6
r7	r7	r7	r7	r7	r7	r7
r8	r8	r8	r8	r8	r8	r8_firq
r9	r9	r9	r9	r9	r9	r9_firq
r10	r10	r10	r10	r10	r10	r10_firq
r11	r11	r11	r11	r11	r11	r11_firq
r12	r12	r12	r12	r12	r12	r12_firq
r13 (SP)	r13 (SP)	r13_svc (SP)	r13_abt (SP)	r13_undef (SP)	r13_irq (SP)	r13_firq (SP)
r14 (LR)	r14 (LR)	r14_svc (LR)	r14_abt (LR)	r14_undef (LR)	r14_irq (LR)	r14_firq (LR)
r15 (PC)	r15 (PC)	r15 (PC)	r15 (PC)	r15 (PC)	r15 (PC)	r15 (PC)

CPSR	CPSR	CPSR	CPSR	CPSR	CPSR	CPSR
		SPSR_svc	SPSR_abt	SPSR_undef	SPSR_irq	SPSR_firq

Alternative register in the considered mode

Figure 3.14. *Organization of register banks according to the Arm® architecture execution mode*

3.1.12.4. *Modes of execution*

Modern microprocessors operate in an execution mode (*cf.* § V4-3.2.2). Two classic modes are the supervisor and user modes. Some flags are available in all modes. Others can only be read and manipulated for certain modes. An example is that of the NS16000. Its status register in format n = 16 bit is called the PSR (Processor Status Register). The least significant byte of this register is called UPSR for user PSR because it is always accessible. The other party's flags are called supervisor flags. In the Pentium II, a register called MSW (Machine Status Word) allows us to know the configuration and the state of the microprocessor. It can be initialized in real and protected modes (level 0 priority) with the smsw (load MSW) instruction. The smsw instruction (MSW store) allows you to read it (with CR4.UMIP[15] = 0 in user mode). In addition, other registers can be accessed differently depending on the mode. The NS16000 has a separate stack pointer, access to which is dependent on an IS/US flag (Interrupt Stack/User Stack). Figure 3.14 shows all of the Arm® architecture registers. Some registers are duplicated for each of the interrupt modes.

3.1.12.5. *Parallelism*

From a programming point of view, register allocation is done by the programmer at the assembly language level or automatically by the High-Level programming Language (HLL) compiler. Internally, a renaming of the registers can take place, allowing the parallel execution of instructions and speculative execution (this will be covered in a future book by the author on microprocessors).

3.1.12.6. *Encoding*

It should be noted that a register allows a simple and unambiguous specification of data dependency because it is specified directly in the instruction code (Oehmke *et al.* 2005) unlike a memory location which can have aliases (*cf.* the concept of virtual memory in V2 on memory function, forthcoming). The use of a small number r of registers (i.e. a few tens) in a microprocessor takes only a few bits in the instruction code ($= \lfloor \log_2(r - 1) \rfloor + 1$ for r > 1 if not 1). It decreases the bus occupancy rate and accelerates access to information. It simplifies the instruction set and the encoding by using only two load-store instructions (RISC approach) for the transfer between short- and long-term memories. The idea of integrating a large number of registers into the microprocessor (Sites 1979) appeared very quickly as soon as advances in microelectronic technology allowed it. This was put into practice with the RISC concept (this will be covered in a future book by the author on microprocessors), an example of use being the windowing of registers (*cf.* § 3.1.11.3).

15 UMIP for User-Mode Instruction Prevention.

Having a large number of registers, that is, a large namespace (register namespace) has an impact on the coding of the instruction (*cf.* § V4-1.1).

3.2. Internal memories

An MPU can have built-in RAM. An example was the MC6802, which had 128×8 bits of RAM on page 0. The interest lies first in a shorter access time than that of an external memory and in the possibility of putting in low-consumption retention when the component is stopped. Access to this zone had priority over an external zone with the same address range.

MPUs in the late 1990s gradually integrated the various levels of cache, starting with the first named L0.

3.3. Integer processing unit

The Integer Processing Unit (IU or IPU), also called arithmetic and logic unit (ALU[16]), can execute arithmetic operations on integers, signed or unsigned, and logical on binary words, under the orders of the Control Unit (CU). Each of them will correspond to an active signal among 2^f (Figure 3.15) coming from the decoding of the instruction code. There are at most two operands per function. The operand can be in a register, a memory or the stack ("Last In, First Out" (LIFO) with constraints related to architecture. It is used implicitly or explicitly (i.e. it is named) in the instruction. The result is framed in n-bit format except in the case of multiplication. After execution, a status is possibly calculated and stored in the flag register (*cf.* § 3.1.5).

The basic arithmetic operations are addition and subtraction. The logical operations are those of combinatorial and sequential logics (*cf.* respectively chapters 2 and 3 of Darche (2002)). Two specific functions of the latter are shift and rotation (*cf.* § V4-2.3.2.3). There will be six basic functions, which are the logical shifts on the left (LSL for Logical Shift Left) and on the right (LSR for Logical Shift Right), arithmetic on the left (ASL for Arithmetic Shift Left) and on the right (ASR for Arithmetic Shift Right) and the rotations to the left (ROL for ROtate Left) and to the right (ROR for ROtate Right). Their number can be reduced to five because the logical and arithmetic shifts to the left are equivalent (LSL = ASL) due to the overwriting of the sign (MSb for Most Significant bit).

---

16 Some processors such as the DSP may also have a calculation unit for floating numbers or FPU (*cf.* § 5.4). The Texas Instruments TMS320C31 is an example. This work will only deal with integers.

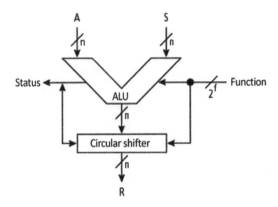

Figure 3.15. *Processing unit with circular shifter*

The shift function is performed by a shifter placed either at the output of the ALU or in front of one of the operand inputs. A shift can be constant or variable. The first case is trivial because it is a simple hardware wiring. To carry out shifts, we saw in § 3.5.3 of Darche (2002) that a network of flip-flops constituting a Shift Register (SR) could be used. But for a reason of speed (time of shift linear function of the number of shifts to be carried out) and also because of the fact that the shift must be done on a single pulse or a clock front, the combinatory version is essential. This is an example which shows that an external operation classically qualified as sequential is not necessarily implemented with operators belonging to sequential logic. The basic approach is to use multiplexers as shown in Figure 3.16. Exercises E3.2 and E3.3 present other examples. A kill value is the logical value, usually 0, inserted at one end of the device in the direction of the shift. This flow diagram performs, on command, a single shift to the left or to the right (bidirectional shifter), hence the two control bits.

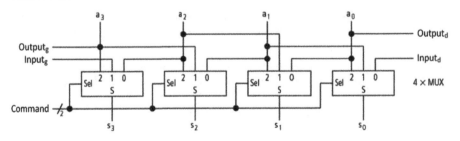

Figure 3.16. *Logical shift of a maximum position in format n = 4 bit*

The rotation function is a shift with looping of its output on its input (circular shift). Recall that a shift or rotation in format n of d bits to the left is equivalent to the same operation to the right of n - $\bar{d}$ bits. In addition to 2^n, this subtraction is therefore equivalent to n + $\bar{d}$ + 1. Moreover, the rotation takes place modulo n.

The two functions are generally combined. The choice "shift or rotation", their number and the direction are specified at the input of the logic system. The device is generally cascadable or iterative (*cf.* § 2.5 of (Darche 2002)); that is, it is possible to combine them in series to increase the working format. To achieve any number of shifts, circular or not, you must have at first approach n multiplexers with n inputs (n:1 MUX). The shift can also be done by an array shifter composed of n columns and d +1 lines. In the example in Figure 3.17, the kill value is shown on the right. All the lines are controlled by a one-active decoder from among n (1:n hot decoder)

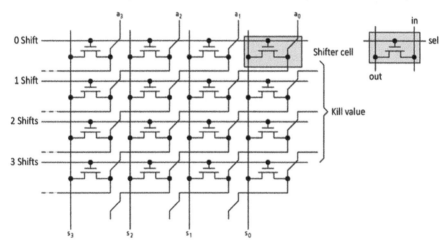

Figure 3.17. *Left array shifter*

The two main shift/rotation structures are the barrel and funnel shifters. The barrel shifter, also called Barrel SWitch (BSW) or circular shifter, is a circuit which is capable of performing a shift at once an arbitrary number of positions. Its name comes from the fact that each input bit can be linked to one of the outputs. So it is very fast. It can be implemented using multiplexers. There are as many as the input format n. Figure 3.18 shows one in format n = 4 bit. This circuit basically rotates right. To perform a rotation, it performs a shift then forces the state of the bits not useful to the kill value (i.e. 0) using a logical mask (masked barrel shifter). The ILLIAC IV computer used such a device in its ALU (Davis 1969). Furthermore, Davis (1974) describes such a circuit in the form of a uniform shift network.

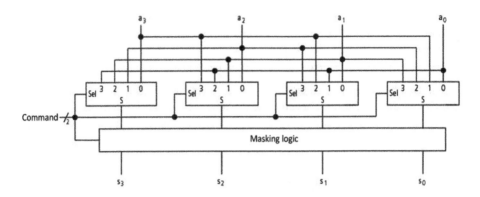

Figure 3.18. *Barrel shifter with logical mask in format n = 4 bit*

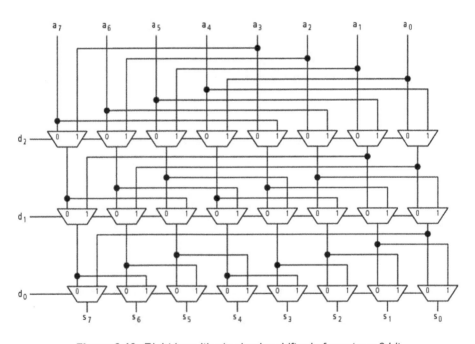

Figure 3.19. *Right logarithmic circular shifter in format n = 8 bit*

The input capacitance and fan-in (*cf.* § 2.2.1 of Darche (2004)) according to the technology used depends on the format n. From an implementation point of view, for electrical and temporal reasons, it is necessary to limit them. Also the number of inputs acceptable for a multiplexer is around four. It is therefore necessary to have several logical levels. A solution which has been proposed is the log(arithmic) shifter composed of $\log_a (n = 2^k)$ levels of multiplexers of type a-to-1 (noted a:1). The interest lies in the absence of a decoder controlling the multiplexers. Figure 3.19 presents a version with 2:1 multiplexers arranged in three logic levels allowing $2^k - 1$ (k = 3) shifts. Bits $d_{2:0}$ control a right shift of 4, 2 and 1 bits respectively.

Figure 3.20 shows the generic version of a barrel shifter in logarithmic version.

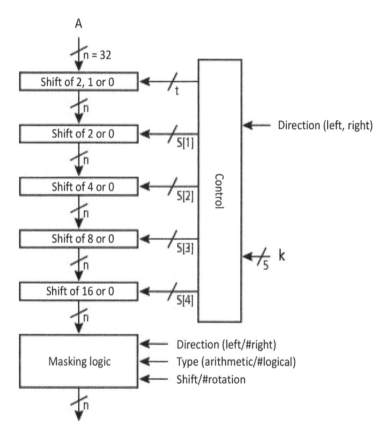

Figure 3.20. *Barrel shifter in logarithmic version*

The basic idea of the funnel shifter is to double the information of word A of format n with the exception of MSb to obtain the source word A' and to select only n consecutive bits (Figure 3.21).

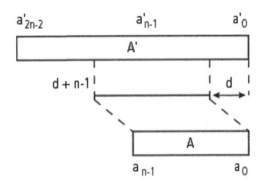

Figure 3.21. *Extraction of the word shifted by d bits from a source word A'*

Table 3.3 specifies the value of the bits of the source word.

Operations	$A'_{2n-2:n}$	A'_{n-1}	$A'_{n-2:0}$	Shift
Logical shift to the right	$a_{n-2:0}$	a_{n-1}	$a_{n-2:0}$	d
Right arithmetic shift	0	a_{n-1}	$a_{n-2:0}$	d
Clockwise rotation	a_{n-1}	a_{n-1}	$a_{n-2:0}$	d
Logical/arithmetic shift to the left	$a_{n-1:1}$	a_0	$a_{n-1:1}$	$\bar{d}$
Left rotation	$a_{n-1:1}$	a_0	0	$\bar{d}$

Table 3.3. *Bit assignment of the source word (from Huntzicker et al. (2008))*

Figure 3.22 presents its logarithmic version.

A unit carrying out several types of instruction will never be faster than several units specializing in one type (Tomasulo 1967). Therefore, it is more interesting to have a separate adder and multiplier than a generalist ALU, regardless of the data representation used. Also, independent specialized units have been installed in the processor as progress has been made in the integration of electronic components. We will then speak for a particular operation of IMUL (Integer MULtiplier) or FMUL (Floating-point MULtiplier) or, more generally of floating-point calculation unit FPU (Floating-Point Unit) or FALU (Floating-Point ALU).

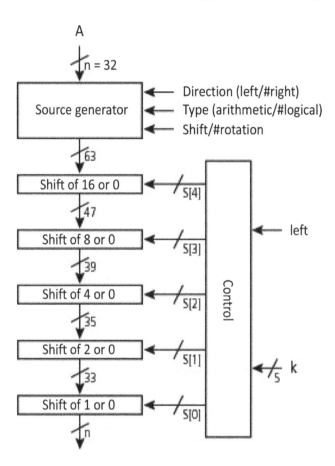

Figure 3.22. *Logarithmic funnel shifter*

3.4. Control unit

The (Computer) Control Unit ((C)CU, (Carter 1995)) or even program control unit (PCU, (Carter 1995)), called in its microprogrammed version, MCU (Microprogram CU), manages the internal units, in particular the IU from instructions of a running program read in the main memory. Its basic functions, four in number, are the search and decoding of the next instruction, the control of the propagation of signals (gating) of the data path for its execution and the change of the state of the system to allow fetching the next instruction as a function, in particular, of status information from the calculation (Figure 3.23).

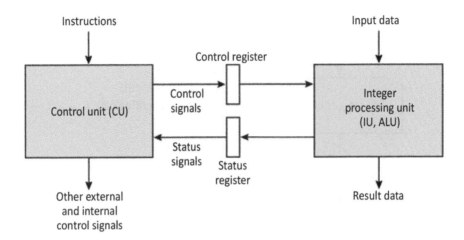

Figure 3.23. *Relationship between control and integer processing units*

3.4.1. *Internal states*

Each instruction executed by the processor gives rise to internal execution in a series of micro-steps or, if the architecture is firmware[17], that is, a series of micro-instructions. This aspect is more particularly detailed in a future book by the author on microprocessors.

Figure 3.24 shows an example of a state transition diagram, that of the 8085. The operation of the MPU is therefore marked by a succession of states. A distinction must be made between so-called internal and external states. The internal state or state of the MPU is the set of information of the MPU, that is, its structured and implemented registers. The external state (to the MPU) is all of the system information except that of the internal state. At the level of program execution, the state of a process (process state) is the set of information relating to the process. It therefore includes the processor state and the part of the external state concerning the process.

---

17 Original meaning of the term "firmware" (FW).

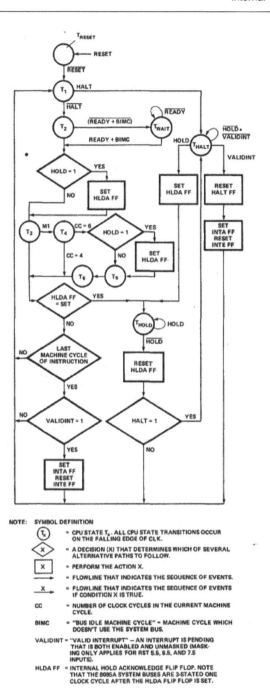

Figure 3.24. *8085A state transition diagram (Intel 1983)*

3.4.2. *Generation of internal synchronization signals*

From a global clock Clk, external or internal to the MPU, h internal synchronization signals ϕ_i (i ∈ [0, h-1]) will be generated to control the different functional subsets as illustrated in Figure 3.25.

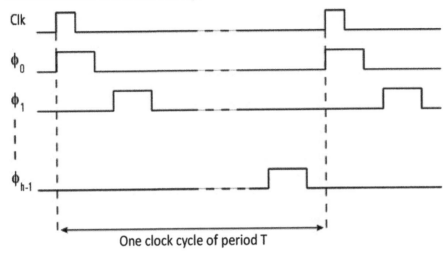

Figure 3.25. *Multi-phase clock signals*

The clock signal Clk qualified as "master" (master clock) actually drives the signal generator (timing generator), which will generate several sub-signals ϕ_0 to ϕ_{h-1}, which will in turn activate a component or a logic subset (Figure 3.26). To generate such a sequence, it is necessary to use a shift register, a counter or a chain of gates (delay line) playing the role of retarder.

Figure 3.27 shows the synchronization signal generator in situation. It cadences the controller which is responsible for commanding the execution of the instructions previously decoded.

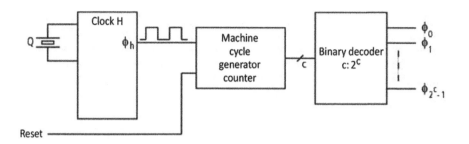

Figure 3.26. *Basic cycle generator*

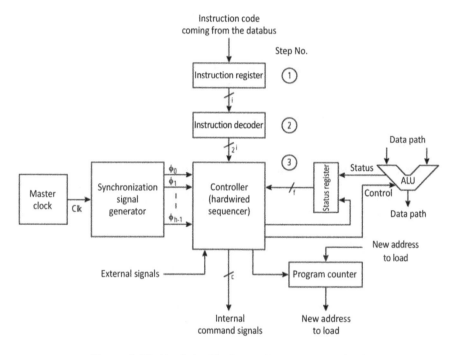

Figure 3.27. *Hardwired logic synchronous control unit*

Hardwired logic and microprogramming are techniques for implementing a central processing unit that functions like a Finite-State Machine (FSM). The implementation can be done with discrete logic, also qualified as random (*cf.* § 4.1 of Darche (2004)). More complex logic components can also be used, such as the multiplexer or the decoder. Today, programmable logic (*cf.* Chapter 4 of Darche (2004)) of PLA type (Programmable Logic Array, *cf.* § 1.2 of Darche (2004)), for example, and random access memories (RAM or ROM (Read-Only Memory), programmable or not) are used. In particular, a non-volatile memory can be used for decoding (*cf.* § 2.2.6 of Darche (2012) and § 2.2.2 of Darche (2003)). These aspects are developed in a future book by the author on microprocessors.

3.4.3. *Phases of the execution cycle*

There are three phases to execute an instruction. For didactic reasons, an instruction will be broken down into an operational field (i.e. operation code) and a reference field, in constant formats c and o respectively (*cf.* § V4-1.1).

3.4.3.1. *Fetch phase*

The first step in the instruction execution cycle is to find the instruction (fetch step) in main memory. This multi-byte word is then stored in the instruction register IR (item 1 in Figure 3.28). Modern MPUs use a hardware pre-fetching step to reduce the latency in accessing instructions.

3.4.3.2. *Decoding phase*

After the fetch phase comes the decoding step (item 2 of Figure 3.28). Its role is to extract information from the instruction code from its various fields. This step indicates, for example, from a function field in f-bit format whose operation is requested in the form of logic signals (2^f-bit format). During this phase, the instruction decoding unit (IDU) must possibly fetch for operands in memory. Ultimately, it initializes the execution sequence.

Figure 3.29 shows a Microprogrammed version. In this type of micro-architecture, the main role of decoding is to determine the starting address of the micro-instruction sequence (i.e. microprogram[18]) corresponding to the instruction from the main memory or from a cache. A read-only memory inserted between the instruction queue and the sequencer makes it possible to address the sequence of the firmware corresponding to the requested instruction (ROM mapping). At this stage, the associated operands are searched and put here in a queue.

---

18 Old meaning of the word "firmware" (*cf.* § V5-3.5.1).

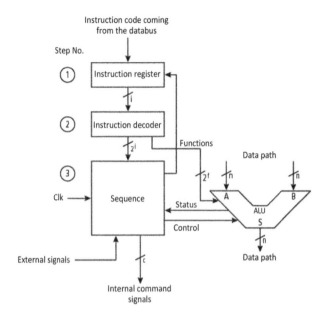

Figure 3.28. *Simplified instruction path (synchronous version)*

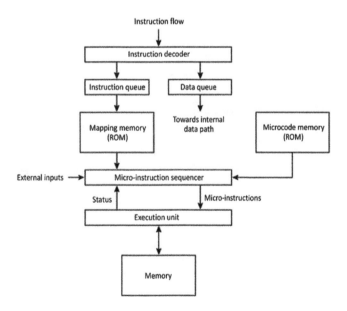

Figure 3.29. *Microprogrammed control unit (inspired by that of the iAPX 432 (Bayliss et al. 1981) and modified)*

The implementation of a decoder can be done in random logic, using a ROM or a programmable logic circuit of PLA type. The memory in the ROM-based decoder serves as a lookup memory. A ROM running the execution is usually large. The decoding operation can be complex, especially in the case of a variable instruction format. It is then necessary to use an FSM. Bayliss *et al.* (1981) and Richardson *et al.* (1981) give an example of a PLA (PLA-based decoder) version for firmware architecture and which concerns the Intel iAPX432 (*cf.* also Kim *et al.* (1993)).

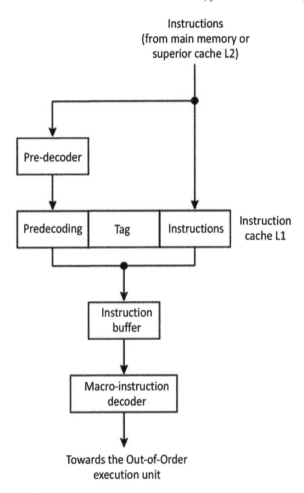

Figure 3.30. *Example of positioning of the pre-decoding in the instruction path*

In post-1990 microprocessors, in order not to increase the cycle time of an instruction, the decoding phase goes through a pre-decoding stage. This new step makes it possible to anticipate certain steps such as the fetch for operands and it facilitates the work of the Instruction Issue Unit (IIU) in ILP (Instruction-Level Parallelism)-type parallel architectures which anticipates actions. Following this step, additional information called pre-decoded bits or tag is then appended to the instruction code to facilitate internal management (Figure 3.30). We see here the interest of integrating the instruction cache in the processor (embedded Synchronous Static RAM (SSRAM)), which allows having more important internal formats. This pre-decoding is carried out by the subset named IPU for instruction predecode unit.

Depending on the processor or rather the ISA, certain instructions may not position the flags, which makes decoding complex. In addition, the format of instructions for modern MPUs with a CISC (Complex Instruction Set Computer) architecture is mostly variable (*cf.* § V4-1.1). These instructions are then stored in memory in a misaligned manner (i.e. framed, *cf.* § 2.6.1 of Darche (2012)). The decoder must first determine the length. It must also operate early to improve the flow of the execution pipelines, for example, by detecting branch instructions. Finally, the decoder contributes 3 to 10% to the energy budget of a modern MPU, in this case of x86-64 bit architecture (Hirki *et al.* 2016). Additional details on all these points will be given in a future book by the author on microprocessors.

3.4.3.3. *Execution phase*

The sequencer then performs processing specific to the requested operation by generating internal control signals intended for the execution unit or IEU (Instruction Execution Unit) and external to the CPU and reacting to the status signals coming from the ALU (item 3 in Figure 3.28). In order for the sequencer to work, a clock signal makes it work. From a control point of view, the fetch and decoding phases are common to all the instructions, but the execution phase is specific (Figure 3.31).

3.4.4. *Other subsets*

The generation of effective addresses (*cf.* § V4-1.2) can be complex because of, in particular, the addressing modes or the virtual memory mechanism. Also a functional subset of the memory manager can be assigned with its own ALU. It is named "Address Generation Unit" (AGU) that can be found in the DSPs (*cf.* § 5.2). It is an element, for example, of the PCU in the DSP56000.

Another subset managed by the CU is the (programmable) interrupt controller or (P)IC responsible for taking into account internal and external interrupt requests, to arbitrate them and generate the corresponding address of the interrupt vector (*cf.* § 4.1.1 of Darche (2004)).

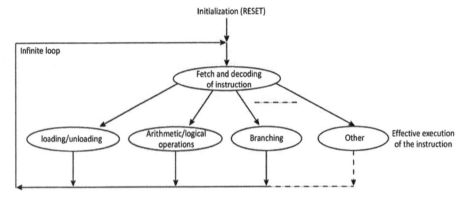

Figure 3.31. *Distribution of the execution (without management of interruption requests)*

3.5. Bus interface

The bus interface initially consisted of simple electronic buffers which logically isolated and electrically amplified the signals from the MPU, their fan-out being too weak (*cf.* § 2.2.1 of Darche (2004)). They have been conventionally called address and memory buffer registers respectively MAR (Memory Address Register) and MDR (or MBR for Memory Data or Buffer Register) and as illustrated in Figure 3.32.

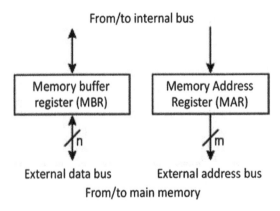

Figure 3.32. *Basic interface of a processor*

Then, access managers with buffering of information (i.e. temporary storage) and access anticipation logic were developed. The BIU (Bus Interface Unit) of the MPU 8086 is responsible for communicating with the outside world in advance. The latter had a 6-byte instruction buffer. There is also the EBI (External Bus Interface) of the PIC32 MCU (MicroController Unit) architecture. This logic module more particularly facilitates the interconnection, via their I/O ports of microcontrollers, of heterogeneous components such as memories or other I/O controllers.

3.6. Note

The functional units of the MPUs including those already presented (CU, IU, BIU) are now working independently and in parallel in order to speed up the execution of instructions.

3.7. Conclusion

This chapter was devoted to the constituents of an MPU. The memory function is mainly entrusted to the registers, the different types of which have been detailed. The integration of a storage area for programming has rarely been proposed, but it is above all the cache levels which today occupy 1/3 or even half the surface of a modern MPU chip (die). The structures of the processing and control units have then been presented.

4

Commercial Microprocessors: From a Single Bit to 128 Bits

This section presents the key characteristics of the first generations of microprocessors or MPU (MicroProcessor Unit). Comparison tables are not exhaustive as they do not cover an entire range. They only cover a representative component of it. Note the evolution of the clocking frequency, the supply voltage and technologies, starting from bipolar then unipolar PMOS (Positive (channel) Metal-Oxide Semiconductor (MOS), *cf.* § 2.1.3 of Darche (2004), NMOS (Negative MOS, *cf.* § 2.1.3 of Darche (2004)) and today CMOS (Complementary MOS). The order of presentation is that of the data processing format or the industrial output time order.

4.1. Single-bit microprocessor

There was a curious single-bit microprocessor introduced in 1977, the MC14500B from Motorola, CMOS technology encapsulated in a 16-pin DIP (Dual-In-Line (DIL) Package, *cf.* § 3.3 of Darche (2004)). It was clocked at about 1 MHz. It was actually an Industrial Control Unit (ICU) called by this same company PLC for Programmable Logic Controller. Its instruction set included 16 instructions. There was no address bus. A memory was addressed sequentially using an external binary counter. Intel, moreover, seems to have associated for an intelligent Input–Output (I/O) controller an 8-bit microprocessor responsible for executing the control program in ROM (Read-Only Memory) integrated and a single bit (Petritz 1977) whose instructions were stored in a programmable logic circuit of PLA type (Programmable Logic Array). Figure 4.1 shows its block diagram.

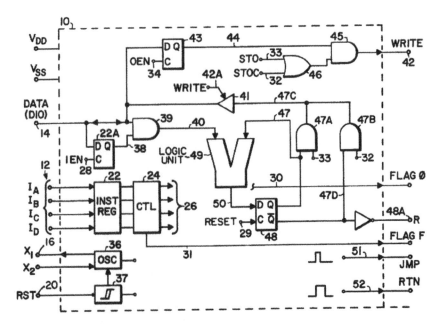

Figure 4.1. *Block diagram of MC14500B (Gregory 1979)*

This type of architecture should not be confused with that of a central unit which works internally at the bit level (serial calculation) but presents a larger format externally. The example is the Datapoint 2200 (*cf.* § 1.2) which, by the way, can be considered as the first microcomputer not equipped with an MPU.

4.2. 4-bit family

The 4-bit family was the first generation. Table 4.1 presents the main characteristics of the first components of this generation. LSI (Large-Scale Integration) manufacturing technology is essentially PMOS, which involves at least two supply voltages.

Characteristics	References		
	4004	4040	PPS-4
Family	MCS-4	MCS-40	PPS-4
Manufacturer	Intel	Intel	Rockwell
Year of introduction	1971	1974	1971
Technology	PMOS	PMOS	PMOS
Number of transistors or technological generation	2,300	3,000	LSI
Number of pins	DIP 16	DIP 24	QIP 42
Initial internal clock frequency (kHz)	740	740	800
Address bus width m (bit)	12	12	12
Physical addressing capacity (bit)	4 Ki × 4	8 Ki × 4	4 Ki × (4 + 4)
Number of addressing modes	4	4	3
Number of instructions	46	60	50
Number of registers	16	24	4
Power supplies (V)	−10/+5	−10/+5	−17

Table 4.1. *Summary characteristics of the main microprocessors of the 4-bit generation*

Figure 4.2 shows the internal architecture of the 4004. It has a single internal data bus. It consists of an ACC (accumulator) register, 16 working registers (MPX registers) and a stack consisting of three 12-bit registers which contain instruction addresses. The MF7114 from the Canadian company Microsystems International Limited (MIL) was designed and produced from this first MPU (Stachniak 2010) and named "the Intel 4005". It was part, with RAM (Random Access Memory) MF7115 and ROM MF1601, of a set of three components referenced MP-1. Three peculiarities for the time were its addressing capacity of 256 KiB, the fact that the eight data registers and the eight 12-bit address registers resided in primary memory and, finally, that the I/O ports were also implemented in main memory. It should be noted that the 4040, an improved version of the 4004, included its entire set of instructions (notion of backward compatibility, *cf.* § V4-3.3.3) to which were added 14 other instructions, in particular of a logical type. The interest of the PPS-4 lies in an internal four-phase clock and a data search in 8-bit format and a few I/O lines as for a microcontroller. Its particular case included four rows of 10, 11, 11 and 10 pins respectively (QIP for Quad-In-Line (QIL) Package). Let us also mention, as a last example, the processor of the PPS-25 series (PPS for Programmed Processor System) from the company Fairchild (1976) made up of two circuits. The first, 3805, was an ALU (Arithmetic and Logic Unit, *cf.* § 3.3), and the second referenced 3806 was the control and function unit.

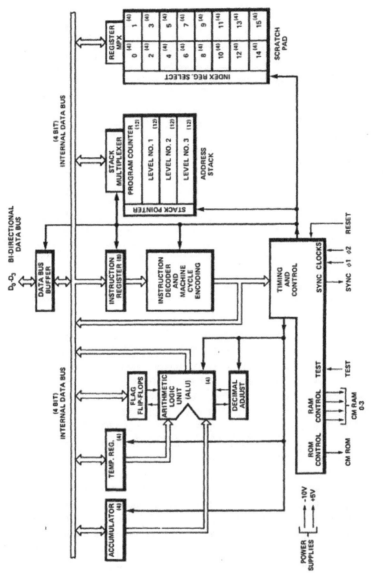

Figure 4.2. Block diagram of the 4004 (Intel 1976)

4.3. 8-bit family

Tables 4.2(a) and 4.2(b) present the characteristics of the main MPU of this family. A feature was their encapsulation in a 40-pin DIP package, with the exception of the 8008, and a register-oriented architecture (*cf.* § V2-3.5.1). Whitworth (1979) distinguishes three generations, the first appeared in 1972 with the 8008, heir to the 4004, the second with the 808x, MC680x and other MCS6502[1] and the last with the 8085, the MC6802/MC6809 and the Z80. The first is characterized by a single internal and external bus, the second by separate address and data buses allowing speed gain (factor of 5 in cycle time (Whitworth 1979)). The addressing capacity is *de facto* "standardized" to the value of 64 KiB. A refinement in this classification by Cushman (1975) and which will be adopted here places the MCS6502, the SC/MP and the EA9002 of the company Electronic Arrays in an intermediate generation (2,5) dating from 1975. This intermediate generation is characterized by improvements such as a generalization of the single supply voltage thanks to the introduction of NMOS and CMOS technologies, an integrated clock circuit or a simplification of the bus control signals.

The 8008 codenamed 1201 is the first 8-bit microprocessor. Figure 4.3 details its internal organization around a single bus. It was used in MICRAL N (*cf.* § 1.2 for a brief history), and for one of the first microcomputers to be built for hobbyists, the Mark-8 (Titus 1974). It included a push-down address call stack with seven address levels, as well as seven scratchpad[2] registers. This stack is well suited for saving/restoring execution contexts.

Its successor, the 8080, is very close from an architectural point of view (Figure V1-3.30). It adds 30 new instructions to the 48 that it shares with its predecessor. They vary in size. Its cycle time is typically 2 μs, an improvement factor of the order of 6. With it, the call stack disappears in favor of a stack pointer which manages the latter in RAM, instead "modern" for all MPUs. The work registers also disappear. It inaugurates the buses of addresses and separate data externally. The program/data and I/O address spaces (*cf.* § 2.1.1.1) are separate.

---

1 This was classified in the third generation by Microcomputer Digest (1975).

2 A working memory or ScratchPad Memory (SPM) is a fast local memory, here a register, which can, for example, temporarily store information for a calculation in progress.

Characteristics	References		
	8008	**8080A**	**MC6800**
Family	MCS-8	MCS-80	MC680x
Generation	1st	2nd	2nd
Manufacturer	Intel	Intel	Motorola
Year of introduction	1972	1974	1974
Technology	PMOS	NMOS	NMOS
Number of transistors or technological generation	3,300	4,500	4,100
Number of pins	DIP 18	DIP 40	DIP 40
Initial internal clock frequency (MHz)	0,5	2	1
Width m of external address bus (bit)	8 (8 + 6, multiplexed with the data bus)	16	16
Physical addressing capacity (bit)	16 Ki × 8	64 Ki × 8	64 Ki × 8
Number of instructions	48	78	72
Number of addressing modes	2	4	7
Number of registers	9	9	6
Power supply (V)	-9/+5	5/+12	+5

Table 4.2(a). *Summary characteristics of the main microprocessors of generations 1 and 2 in 8-bit format*

Characteristics	References		
	CDP1802	MCS6502	ISP-8A/500D
Family	COSMAC	MCS6500	SC/MP (SCAMP)
Generation	2nd	2nd,5th	2nd,5th
Manufacturer	RCA	MOS technology	NS
Introductory year	1975	September 1975	1976
Technology	CMOS	NMOS	PMOS then NMOS
Number of transistors or technological generation	5,000	3,510	LSI
Number of pins	DIP 40	DIP 40	DIP 40
Initial internal clock frequency (MHz)	0,3125 @ +5V	1	1
Width m of external address bus (bit)	8 (16 multiplexed)	16	12
Physical addressing capacity (bit)	64 Ki × 8	64 Ki × 8	64 KiB in16 pages of 4 KiB
Number of instructions	91	56	46
Number of addressing modes	4	11	4
Number of registers	18	6	7
Power supply (V)	+3 / 15	+5	+5

Table 4.2(b). *Summary characteristics of the main microprocessors of generations 1 and 2 in 8-bit format (continued)*

Its main competitor was the MC6800 with three internal buses (*cf.* § V1-3.4.1) and a single address space. I/O is projected into memory, therefore contrary to Intel's philosophy. Its prototype in microprogrammed version included 451 classic TTL (Transistor–Transistor Logic) boxes of the gate and flip-flop type on five printed circuits (Altman 1974), and the chip integrates the equivalent of 120 TTL MSI (Medium-Scale Integration) Integrated Circuit (Young *et al.* 1974). The use of NMOS technology allows a single external +5 V supply with an internal positive voltage doubler (Buchanan 1976) to make a second positive voltage. Its 72 instructions vary in size.

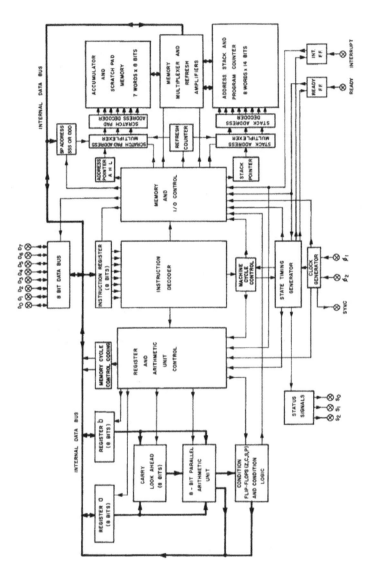

Figure 4.3. *Block diagram of 8008 (Intel 1972)*

The RCP (Radio Corporation of America) CDP1802 is part of the COSMAC (Complementary Symmetry Monolithic Array Computer) family (Winder 1974). It was the first MPU to use CMOS technology. Its static logic made it possible to stop its operation (f_{clock} = 0 Hz). It had an R table of 16 16-bit format scratchpad registers, that is, for general (and temporary) use for data or to have one of three specific functions. Thus, the PC (Program Counter, *cf.* § 3.1.3) can be any register thanks to a register designator P in 4-bit format, in the instruction code, which allows us to designate it, R(0) being at initialization the ordinal counter.

The register X in the same format designates which register points to the operand in memory. Register N performs five functions (RCA 1975). Two of them are used to initialize the two previous registers. It designates one of the registers in the table for a register operation. It is used during an I/O operation to give a command or selection code for a device. Finally, it indicates a UAL operation or a type of conditional test. This choice of architecture is interesting for having rapid context switches. It was used in space as a control processor due, among other things, to its low consumption and resistance to radiation in the MAGSAT satellite launched in 1979 and the Galileo probe launched in 1989.

The MCS6501, predecessor of the MCS6502, was compatible with the MC6800 at pin and bus level (*cf.* § V4-3.3.1), but this first component was withdrawn from the market due to an industrial law dispute on the part of from Motorola. The company Apple was one of the first companies to integrate the MCS6502 into its famous microcomputers Apple I and especially II (*cf.* § V5-3.1). Then, there were the Commodore 64 machines, Nintendo Entertainment System and the Atari 2600 game console.

The SC/MP[3] for Simple Cost-effective Chip MicroProcessor (NS 1976) presented directional buses (Figure 4.4). It should be noted that, despite its addressing capacity of 64 KiB, the address bus was 12 bits wide. It did not have a dedicated stack pointer register but three pointer registers (PTR[3:0] for PoinTer Register) who's PTR0 fulfills the function of PC. It should be noted, extremely rare case, that it incremented the PC before fetching the instruction, which means that the address of the first instruction on initialization (i.e. after a reset) was 0001_{16}. Three signals of bus management BREQ (Bus REQuest), ENIN and ENOUT allowed realizing a multiprocessor system, exceptional functionality for the time.

---

3 Pronounced *scamp*.

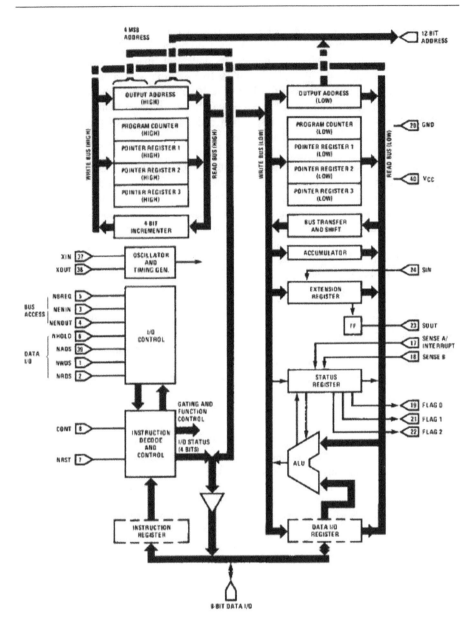

Figure 4.4. *Functional diagram of the INS8060 (SC/MP in NMOS version) (NS 1978)*

Table 4.3 shows the third and the last generation. The Z80 innovated with a refresh logic (mechanism described in § 5.2.2 of Darche (2012) necessary for Dynamic RAM or DRAM) integrated. It had a high number of addressing modes. Its instruction set included that of the 8080, hence a high cardinality. Its static logic makes it possible to stop the processor.

Characteristics	References			
	Z80	**8085A**	**MC6802**	**MC6809**
Family	-	MCS-85	MC680x	MC680x
Generation	3rd	3rd	3rd	3rd
Manufacturer	Zilog	Intel	Motorola	Motorola
Year of introduction	1976	1977	mars 1977	1979
Technology	NMOS	HMOS	NMOS	NMOS
Number of transistors	8,000	6,500	11,000	9,000
Number of pins	DIP 40	DIP 40	DIP 40	DIP 40
Initial internal clock frequency (MHz)	2.5	3	1	1
Width m of external address bus (bit)	16	16	16	16
Physical addressing capacity (bit)	64 Ki × 8	64 Ki × 8	64 Ki × 8	64 Ki × 8
Number of instructions	158	113	72	59
Number of addressing modes	10	4	7	9
Number of registers	$6 + (2 \times 8)$	10	6	9
Power supply (V)	+5	+5	+5	+5

Table 4.3. *Summary characteristics of the main 8-bit microprocessors of third generation*

The instruction set for the 8085A included that of its predecessor, the 8080A, adding to the 113 two new ones, sim and rim. Binary compatibility is ensured. It included its two peripheral circuits, the clock signal generator 8224 and the bus amplifiers 8228 or 8238. The address and data buses, on the other hand, are multiplexed on the least significant 8 bits. The management of interruptions is simplified.

The microprocessors MC6802 and MC6809 (*cf.* a presentation in Powers (1978)) presented an upward compatibility of the source code (*cf.* § V4-3.3.3) with the MC6800, with regard to the instruction set and the addressing modes. The MC6809 control logic is of the "hard-wire logic" type. This component offered wired multiplication, a guarantee of speed of calculation.

4.4. 12-bit family

There are not only families that process integers in format n which is a power of 2. The circuits referenced IM6100 and IM6120 from the company Intersil and manufactured in CMOS technology (Thomas 1976) are two examples. Its instruction set was compatible (*cf.* § V4-3.3.2) with the PDP-8 from DEC (DEC). The TLCS12 from Toshiba in NMOS technology is a second example (Ogdin 1975; Mori *et al.* 1977).

4.5. 16-bit family

The 16-bit generation marks a turning point because technology makes it possible to implement high-level concepts such as the (primary) memory protection offered, for example, by virtual memory (mechanism detailed in the second work on microprocessors) and the supervisor execution mode, these protections being necessary for modern operating systems (*cf.* § V4-3.2.2).

The first generation dates from 1974 with the IPC-16A/520 from the PACE (Processing and Control Element) family from NS in PMOS technology. The first two versions in NMOS technology are the CP1600 and the TMS 9900. The CP1600 has 8 Ri registers (i ∈ [0, 7]), the last two of which are SP (Stack Pointer) and PC respectively. A special feature is that these eight registers are also accessible as simple registers for general use. There are also no specific stack handling instructions, and the management of the R6 register (SP) is implicit when accessing the stack, decrementing or incrementing being done according to the type of access (i.e. read or write). It should be noted that, unlike the majority, the TMS 9900 has a memory–memory architecture (*cf.* § V1-3.5.1). Only three internal registers are used to manage the machine. In particular, the WP register (Workspace Pointer, *cf.* § 3.1.1) points to a set of 16 registers in primary memory. This component emulates the instruction set of Data General's NOVA series minicomputers. The technology of the 9440 Microflame™ is bipolar. It offers, with its 50 instructions and its eight addressing modes, 2,192 possible operation codes compatible with NOVA1200. Table 4.4 summarizes the main characteristics of these MPUs.

Characteristics	References			
	IPC-16A/520	CP1600	TMS 9900	9440
Family	PACE	1600	TMS 9900	MICROFLAME™
Manufacturer	NS	General Instruments	TI	Fairchild
Year of introduction	1974	1975	1976	1977
Technology	PMOS	NMOS	NMOS	I^3L
Number of transistors or technological generation	LSI	LSI	8,000	LSI
Number of pins	CERDIP[4] 40	CERDIP 40	DIP 64	CERDIP 40
Initial internal clock frequency (MHz)	1,333	5	3	10
Width m of external address bus (bit)	16	16 multiplexed	15	15 multiplexed
Physical addressing capacity (bit)	64 Ki words	64 Ki words	64 Ki words	64 Ki words
Number of instructions	45	87	69	50
Number of addressing modes	5	3	7	8
Number of registers	7	8	3	8
Power supply (V)	-12/+5/+8	-3/+5/+12	5/+12	+5

Table 4.4. *Summary characteristics of the main 16-bit microprocessors of the first generation*

The tendency of the second generation is to support high-level languages with complex instructions and additional data types. The 8088, version of the 8086 with an external 8-bit interface, is the MPU chosen by IBM for its Personal Computer (PC). The 8088/8086 introduces the segmentation of main memory, one of the mechanisms with the paging of virtual memory. They also have a fetch-ahead buffer respectively 4 and 6 bytes in size. The 256 possible interruptions are vectorized (*cf.* § V4-5.7). The Intel company with the 80286 introduced two modes of execution (*cf.* § V4-3.2.2), real and protected, with the defect that it was necessary to do a reset to return to the real mode. The MC68000[5] was the first microprocessor for workstations like the first from

---

4 For CERamic DIP.

5 Its designation refers to its number of transistors and also to its predecessor, the MC6800.

Sun or Silicon Graphics or Lisa microcomputers and the first Apple Macintoshes. Its particularity was to have internal registers in 32-bit format, and it had two modes of execution, user and supervisor. Z8000 family microprocessors are not compatible with the Z80 architecture. The memory management of the Z8001 is segmented, unlike the Z8002. It has two execution modes, normal (i.e. user) and system. Table 4.5 summarizes the main characteristics of these components.

Characteristics	References			
	8086	MC68000	Z8001	80286
Family	x86	68K	Z8000	x86
Manufacturer	Intel	Motorola	Zilog	Intel
Year of introduction	1978	1979	1979	1982
Technology	NMOS then HMOS	HMOS	NMOS	MOS
Number of transistors	29,000	68,000	17,500	134,000
Number of pins	DIP 40	DIP 64	DIP 48	PGA[6]/LCC[7] 68
Initial internal clock frequency (MHz)	5	8	4	6
Width m of external address bus (bit)	20	16	16	16
Physical addressing capacity (bit)	1 Mi × 8	16 Mi × 8	8 Mi × 8	16 Mi × 8
Number of instructions	95	56	110	103
Number of addressing modes	24	14	8	8
Number of registers	14	16	20	15
Number of execution modes or names	1	user/supervisor	normal/system	real/protected
Power supply (V)	+5	+5	+5	+5

Table 4.5. *Summary characteristics of the main 16-bit microprocessors of second generation*

4.6. 32 bits

The 32-bit generation appeared from the early 1980s. It marks the transition to the complementary MOS technology (i.e. CMOS). Two architectures marked the 1980s.

6 For Pin Grid Array (Package).
7 For (ceramic) Leadless Chip Carrier.

The first is called RISC (Reduced Instruction Set Computer). The second is Instruction-Level Parallelism (ILP). The RISC approach consists mainly and, as the name suggests, of reducing the number of instructions to the bare minimum and optimizing their execution. It comes in opposition to the CISC (Complex Instruction Set Computer) approach. The parallelism in the instructions comes from research that began during the late 1960s–early 1970s (Jouppi 1989). It brings together techniques for designing families of processors and compilers to break with sequential execution. It was first implemented in supercomputers and mainframe computers. Then, these techniques appeared in microprocessors from the 1980s to accelerate the execution of instructions, more particularly those relating to the transfer between CPU and main memory (and vice versa) and to arithmetic calculations for whole and floating numbers. Increasing performance means executing more than one instruction per processor cycle (i.e. IPC (Instructions Per Cycle) > 1, cf. § V4-3.4). We must distinguish three paths, the pipeline, the static and dynamic superscalar approaches and the VLIW (Very Long Instruction Word, cf. § 4.7) architecture. They will be studied in a future book by the author on microprocessors. Tables 4.6(a) and 4.6(b) summarize the main characteristics of the components of this generation.

Characteristics	References			
	NS32032	**MC68020**	**R2000**	**MB86900**
Family	NS32000	68000	MIPS I	SPARC V7
Manufacturer	NS	Motorola	MIPS	Fujitsu
Year of introduction	1984	1984	1986	1987
Technology	CMOS	HCMOS[8]	CMOS	CMOS
Number of transistors	70,000	180,000	110,000	110,000
Number of pins	68 LCC	PGA 114 /QFP[9] 132	PGA 144	PGA 256
Initial internal clock frequency (MHz)	10	16.67	12.5	16.67
Architecture	CISC	CISC	RISC	RISC
Width m of external address bus (bit)	32	32	32	32
Physical addressing capacity (bit)	16 MiB = 2^{24}	4 GiB = 2^{32}	2^{32}	4 Gi words

---

8 For High-speed CMOS.

9 For Quad Flat Package.

Characteristics	References			
	NS32032	**MC68020**	**R2000**	**MB86900**
Logical addressing capacity (bit)	No internal MMU	No internal MMU	$2^{31} \times 8$	No internal MMU
Number of instructions	> 107	> 103	74	55
Number of addressing modes	9	18	3	2
Number of registers	16	18	32	120
Execution mode names	User/supervisor	User/supervisor	User/supervisor	User/supervisor
Power supply (V)	+5	+5	+5	+5

Table 4.6(a). *Summary characteristics of the main 32-bit microprocessors*

The virtual (or logical) memory manager or MMU (Memory Management Unit, this will be covered in a future book by the author on memories) is starting to be integrated into the chip (Table 8.6(b)).

Characteristics	References		
	80386DX	**80486DX**	**PowerPC™ 601**
Family	x86	x86	PowerPC™
Manufacturer	Intel	Intel	Motorola/IBM
Year of introduction	1988	April 1989	1993
Technology	CHMOS III	CHMOS IV	CMOS
Number of transistors	275,000	1,180,000	2,800,000
Number of pins	132 PGA/QFP	CPGA[10] 168	CPGA 304
Initial internal clock frequency (MHz)	20	25/33	50
Architecture	CISC	CISC	RISC superscalar
Width m of external address bus (bit)	32	32	32

---

10 For Ceramic PGA (Package).

Physical addressing capacity (bit)	4 GiB	4 GiB	4 PiB $= 2^{32} \times 8$
Logical addressing capacity (bit)	64 TiB $= 2^{32} \times 2^{14} \times 8$	64 TiB $= 2^{32} \times 2^{14} \times 8$	4 PiB $= 2^{52} \times 8$
Number of instructions	128	> 150	272
Number of addressing modes	11	11	3
Number of registers	16	16	115
Execution mode names	Real/protected/8086 virtual	Real/protected/8086 virtual	User/supervisor
Power supply (V)	+5	+5	+3.6

Table 4.6(b). *Summary characteristics of the main 32-bit microprocessors*

The NS32032 (NS16000 family renamed in May 1984) is inspired by the VAX™ architecture with addressing modes and additional registers as well as modifications to the instruction set. It implements the paging mechanism.

The MC68020, described by Gay (1984) and MacGregor *et al.* (1984), is the 32-bit version (i.e. internal and external data paths and registers in this format) of the MC68000. Its different buses are not multiplexed. Figure 4.5 shows its block diagram.

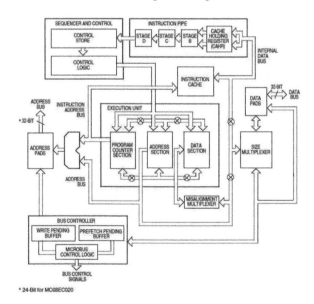

Figure 4.5. *MC68020/EC020 block diagram (Motorola 1992)*

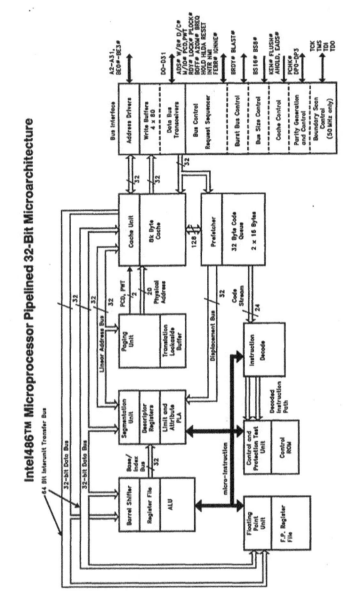

Figure 4.6. *Block diagram of the i486™ (Intel 1992)*

Unlike the previous two, the R2000 (Moussouris *et al.* 1986; Kane 1988) has a RISC architecture. It is the first industrial component of MIPS (Microprocessor without Interlocked Pipeline Stages) architecture (Hennessy *et al.* 1982b), an academic research project started in 1981 at Stanford University (USA). The SPARC architecture for Scalable Processor ARChitecture (Sun 1987; Garner *et al.* 1988; Hitchcock 1990; Agrawal and Garner 1992), also RISC-inspired, dates from 1986. The first implementations were the MB86900 from the company Fujitsu (Quach and Chueh 1988) and CY7C601 from Cypress (Namjoo 1989).

Furthermore, the Intel architecture continues the development of its family with backward compatibility (*cf.* § V4-3.3.3) with the 386 (El-Ayat and Agarwal 1985; Crawford 1986) and the 486 (Fu *et al.* 1990). These two components offer three execution modes named real, protected with four privilege levels and virtual 8086, and they have the same logical and physical addressing capabilities. The 486 integrates for the first time in this family an L1 cache of 8 KiB and a mathematical coprocessor (DX version, *cf.* Figure 4.6). Six instructions are added (`bswap`, `cmpxchg`, `xadd`, `invd`, `wbinvd` and `invlpg`, *cf.* the next volume). The last three are used to manage internal caches.

The PPC 601 is the first implementation of the RISC PowerPC™ architecture (PC for Performance Computing), itself derived from the POWER architecture (Oehler and Groves 1990) (POWER for Performance Optimization With Enhanced RISC), originally intended for RS/6000 workstations (RS for RISC System). It also has an integrated FPU (Floating-Point Unit, *cf.* § 5.4). Becker *et al.* (1993) and Moore (1993) describe this component, the block diagram of which is presented in Figure 4.7.

4.7. New generations

Under this title are gathered the new trends which are multithreading architectures and multicore in 32- or 64-bit format of the 1990s (at the research level). During this period, the classic ILP approach in MPUs showed its limits. After increasing the processor clocking frequency and after exploiting parallelism at the cycle level with the pipeline and superscalar approaches, VLIW or EPIC (Explicitly Parallel Instruction Computing) was proposed Thread-Level Parallelism (TLP), in particular, SMT (Simultaneous MultiThreading) and hyper-threading (Tullsen *et al.* 1995, 1996) consisting of transforming parallelism at thread level into a parallelism at the instruction level. This allowed the progression of computing power to continue. Another approach is to run multiple light processes or threads during a cycle. The implementing component is called "multithreaded processor" and the associated technology, CMT for Chip MultiThreading. Large companies such as IBM, Intel and Sun have proposed components that implement the latter. CMT technology is detailed in hardware multithreading or HMT for Hardware MultiThreading and in multicore approach or CMP (Chip MultiProcessing). The HMT approach is based on processor cores running multiple threads (multithreaded cores). On this subject, *cf.* Ungerer *et al.*

(2003). To finish, let us quote some emblematic architectures of processors like Alpha AXP (McLellan 1993; Sites 1993) of Digital Equipment (Compaq), SPARC V9 (Weaver and Germond 1994, 2000) of Sun Microsystems and POWER3 (O'Connell and White 2000) and superior. All these concepts and components will be studied in the third work on microprocessors.

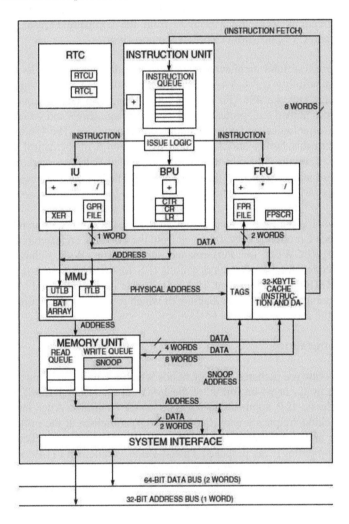

Figure 4.7. *Block diagram of the PowerPC™ 601 (Motorola 1993)*

NOTE.– This § illustrated in § V1-3.4.3.

4.8. Conclusion

This chapter presented the different families of MPUs according to their internal working format. The architectures from the 16-bit format will be detailed in the following works.

5

Special Cases

The microprocessor or MPU (MicroProcessor Unit) has been produced industrially in various versions to adapt to specific fields. Thus, we mainly find the bit-slice processor, digital signal processor, microcontroller and parallelism processors.

5.1. Bit-slice processor

For more performance and customization, the sliced approach was proposed. The idea was to split the central unit in width, that is, in bits rather than functionally (i.e. Arithmetic and Logic Unit (ALU), Control or Command Unit (CU), registers, etc.). A processor then consists of several bit slices, a slice generally comprising 2, 4 or 8 bits. Manufacturers supplied standard components such as the Macrologic™ family from Fairchild (Rallapalli and Verhofstadt 1975; Fairchild 1976). It is therefore not a microprocessor within the meaning of the definition in § 1.1, that is, a single component but instead had all the functionality. The major advantage is the possibility of fixing the working format of the processor to adapt it to the target application. The disadvantages were the number of Integrated Circuit (IC) packages proportional to the number of slices and, consequently, higher power consumption compared to that of a monolithic solution (i.e. MPU in a single package). Their main area of use was signal processing. The emblematic circuit was the AMD 2900 4-bit format circuit manufactured in TTL (Transistor–Transistor Logic) S[1] series technology. Let us also mention the 3000 series (format n = 4 bits) from the company Intel (second source: Signetics) and Motorola's 10800 respectively of TTL and ECL (Emitter Coupled Logic) technologies, both bipolar. The sliced solution no longer

---

1 For Schottky, two components are concerned, the diode (schottky-barrier or hot-carrier diode) and the transistor (schottky (clamped) transistor).

exists commercially with the progress of integration. The multiprocessor solution, that is, the multiplication of cores or MPUs, was preferred.

5.2. Digital signal processor

The Digital Signal Processor (DSP) is integrated into a signal processing chain shown in Figure 5.1. It mainly consists of Analog/Digital Converter (ADC) and Digital/Analog Converter (DAC, *cf.* § 3.5.1 of Darche (2003)) and the DSP. Upstream of the acquisition, there is a possible preamplifier, the anti-aliasing low-pass filter and the sample-and-hold circuit, the latter then allowing the quantization (discretization) of a stable signal by the converter. Downstream of the DAC, the anti-aliasing low-pass filter removes the sampling frequency. Multiplexers (MUX) allow you to process multiple sources and demultiplexers (DMUX) allow you to have multiple outputs.

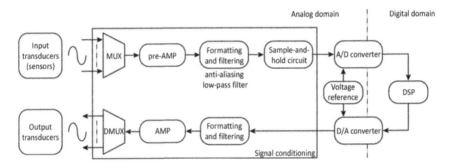

Figure 5.1. *Digital signal processing chain ((Darche 2003) modified)*

Figure 5.2 shows the different signal forms encountered during the acquisition phase. The analog input signal (Figure 5.2(a)) is first sampled and its value held (Figure 5.2(b)). Each sample is then quantified, that is, measured (Figure 5.2(c)). Quantization allows the discretization of the amplitude values of the signal. The amplitude of the signal, which was a continuous function, then becomes a set of discrete values, that is, a digital set. The representation of the numbers used is, in almost all cases, that with fixed point (*cf.* § II.4.1 of Darche (2000)) for calculations with numbers with point and, moreover, mostly in real-time.

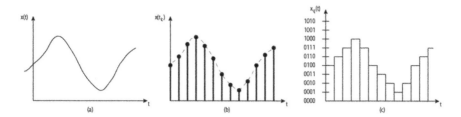

Figure 5.2. *Steps to convert an analog signal*

Figure 5.3 summarizes the four forms of a signal according to the amplitude and the time considered. Times and amplitudes can be continuous or discrete in nature.

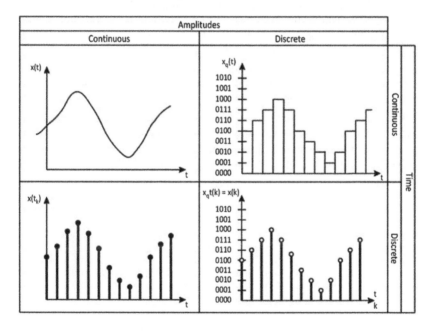

Figure 5.3. *The four families of signals (from Kunt (1981))*

From sampled continuous signals, digital processing can be carried out, in real-time or not. Representative examples of processing are filtering, convolution (mixing of two signals), correlation (comparison of two signals), amplitude, phase or frequency (de)modulation, audio/video (de)compression, detection/correction of error(s). In particular, the audio processing is noise reduction, equalization, echo cancellation and frequency conversion. It allows spectral analysis of a signal, for example, by (Fast) Fourier Transform (FFT).

The equations that a DSP calculates for e, f and m samples are generally of two types:

$$\sum_{i=0}^{e-1} a_i \times x(n-i) \qquad\qquad [5.1]$$

$$y(n) = \sum_{i=0}^{f-1} a_i \times x(n-i) + \sum_{k=1}^{m} b_k \times y(n-k) \qquad\qquad [5.2]$$

where, at time n, $y(n)$ is the current value of the output sample; $y(n-k)$ are the past values of the output samples; $x(n)$ is the current value of the input sample; $x(n-k)$ are the past values of the input samples; and a_i and b_k are the coefficients associated with the filter. The first equation is that of a Finite Impulse Response (FIR) filter. The value of the output sample $y(n)$ depends only on the previous values of the input samples $x(n-i)$. The second is that of an Infinite Impulse Response (IIR) filter. To calculate them, certain instructions are specialized such as multiplication/addition (Multiply-and-ACcumulate or mac, $AC \leftarrow AC + (operand\_1 \times operand\_2)$) which is executed like many others in a single cycle, sign of computing power. This operation is also called merged multiplication–addition or FMA for Fused Multiply-Add or Multiply-Accumulate or FMAC for Fused MAC operation. It is included in the IEEE 754-2008 standard (IEEE 2008). The MAC unit ((Multiply-and-ACcumulate unit), also called the MAF unit (Multiply-Add-Fused unit) specialized in the execution of this mac instruction, is a specificity of this component. The von Neumann architecture is not in fact suitable for this type of calculation since it would be done in two stages: it consists basically of a multiplier, an adder and an AC (accumulator) register (Figure 5.4).

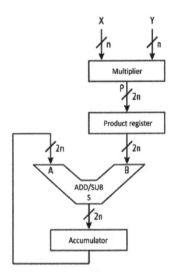

Figure 5.4. *Basic MAC unit*

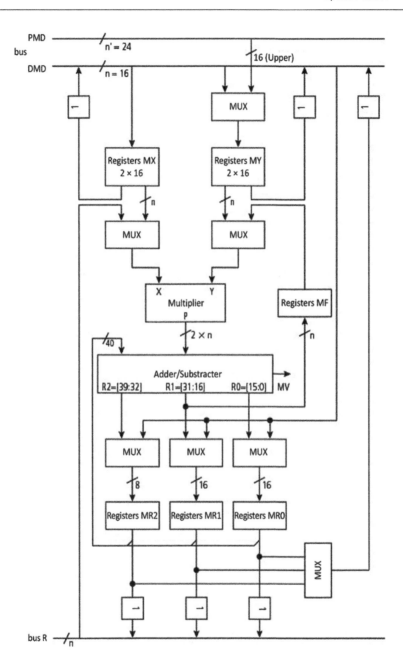

Figure 5.5. *Block diagram of ADSP-2104 from Analog Devices*

The first integrated unit of this type was that of the IBM POWER1 (Grohoski 1990; Oehler and Groves 1990), the GPP-type processor (General-Purpose Processor, *cf.* § 1.1) equipping RISC (Reduced Instruction Set Computer) System/6000, hence the acronym RS/6000, working in a floating point representation described in Hokenek *et al.* (1990) and Montoye *et al.* (1990). Figure 5.5 shows the simplified block diagram of the ADSP-2104 from Analog Devices.

More generally, the instructions are implemented for whole numbers and, for the most powerful components, floating points. This type of processor uses for the calculation a saturated arithmetic rather than the classic modular arithmetic which can cause calculation errors because of format overrun or overflow.

The DSP has a complex address generator or DAG (Data Address Generator). It provides the address for accessing information (data or instruction). It can auto increment the stored address after the execution of an instruction (post-modification), a transfer, for example. It can modify it beforehand (pre-modification) for a transfer without changing it in memory later. It can also modify it without making a transfer. Finally, it can provide a modified address, for example, a reverse address (bit-reverse address), without modifying it in memory. Figure 5.6 shows the processing order when calculating the address.

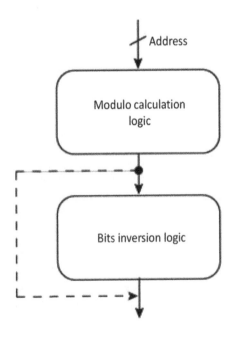

Figure 5.6. *Chain of address processing*

Furthermore, there is no zero-overhead loop thanks to the presence of three registers, one as a counter and the other two to store the start and end addresses of the block to be repeated, thereby removing the branch instruction. The management of the loop is therefore material (*cf.* § V4-2.4.3 for details of the structure).

We can therefore qualify this component as a SISC (Special Instruction Set Computer, *cf.* § V1-3.4.3.1) (Madisetti 1995) which is characterized by addressing the methods adapted to its field of applications such as circular and reverse bit addressing (*cf.* § V4-1.2.4.5) and specialized instructions in the field such as mac.

What also differentiates the digital signal processing of a microprocessor for general use is its architecture called the classic or better yet modified Harvard (from the name of the university, *cf.* § V1-3.4.2) architecture which is characterized by a memory for instructions and one for data and, for the modified version, by another data bank. The interest lies in the ability to fetch two pieces of data in a single cycle. There are therefore two data buses. The conventional microprocessor is a register-oriented processor, while the DSP is a memory-oriented processor. Like any modern processor, a DSP has fast RAM (Random Access Memory) and a hierarchy of built-in caches.

The DSPs then multiplied the number of calculation units (component example: DSP16000 from Lucent). Figure 5.7 shows the internal architecture of a DSP. This component has five internal buses which are the address and data memory program buses respectively PMA (Program Memory Address) and PMD (Program Memory Data) bus, the address and data buses of the program memory respectively DMA (Data Memory Address) and DMD (Data Memory Data) bus and, finally, the result bus (R bus) which interconnects the computing units. These are the classic ALU and two other specialized computing units which are the MAC unit and the shifter. They then evolved towards the architecture with a very long instruction word (VLIW, *cf.* § 4.7) with, for example, a 256-bit instruction word like the TMS320C62x from the company Texas Instruments (TI, search packet of eight 32-bit instruction words). This type of processor was first programmed in assembly language (*cf.* § V5-1.3) to make the best use of microarchitecture. Today, architecture like VLIW requires programming in a High-Level programming Language (HLL), most often C.

Sometimes, Input–Output (I/O) controllers can be integrated as a serial communication port, a parallel port or, more specialized for signal processing, an A/D converter and one of type D/A. Today's DSP (2010) incorporates the classic features of modern microprocessors such as low power mode or multiprocessing. It also offers functions such as PWM (Pulse Width Modulation) specific to the microcontroller. Like any modern processor, it integrates a JTAG interface (Joint Test Action Group, *cf.* § V5-2.2.5) for debugging. Outside of its field of application, it is generally slower than a conventional processor! The DSP is also available in a microcontroller version (*cf.* § 5.3).

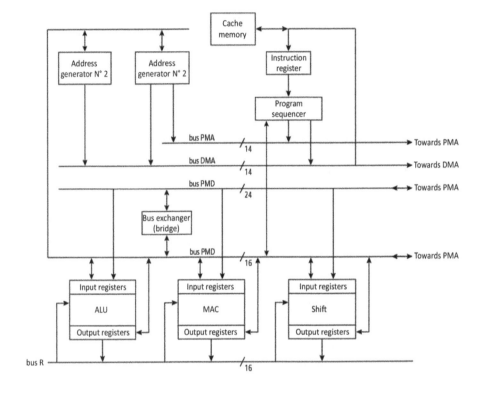

Figure 5.7. *ADSP-2100 internal architecture (based on Analog Device (1990))*

As Figure 5.8 illustrates, a simple digital signal processing system has two memories, one for the program and one for the data. They communicate with the DSP by separate buses. I/O controllers allow signal input and output. This type of processor massively obviously uses DMA (Direct Memory Access) mode for data transfers.

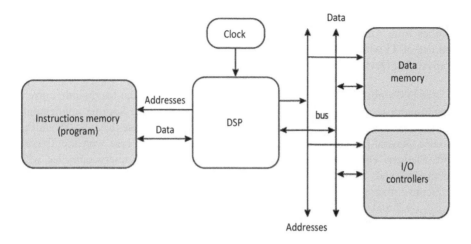

Figure 5.8. *Generic architecture of a DSP-based system*

A digital processing system is less sensitive to its environment (temperature, humidity, etc.) and to aging which, in analog electronics, causes drifts of electrical and time characteristics of the components. Indeed, an electronic component, whether passive or active, has its electrical and temporal characteristics which fluctuate as a function of physical parameters such as temperature, voltage, etc. or time (aging). It is programmable and allows rapid evolution by a simple change of software (SW). It requires no adjustment except initially, for example, for a closed-loop control. Behavior is reproductive and predictive.

The fields of use are wired and cellular telecommunications, speech processing (synthesis and recognition), 2D and 3D images (D for dimensions), multimedia, control (motor control, for example) and instrumentation (FFT analyzer, spectrum analyzer, digital oscilloscope (DSO for Digital Storage Oscilloscope), etc.).

The first DSP in a single chip (monochip) on the market was the µPD7720 from the Japanese company NEC introduced in 1980. It should be noted that a signal processor despite its qualification as analog (analog signal processor) referenced 2920 by the company Intel developed by Marcian E. Hoff and Matt Townsen and introduced in 1979 allowed digital processing of a signal. This component included two converters, one analog/digital and the other digital/analog. Another circuit to mention is the AMI S2811 announced in 1978 which was a DSP-type controller. Then came the TMS32010 offered by the company TI in 1982 (Magar *et al.* 1982). The market is dominated by the company TI (65% in 2007) followed by the companies Freescale (e.g. Motorola, 12% in 2007) and Analog Devices (Forward Concepts 2008). Iconic representatives were the TMS320 (Frantz 1986; Lin *et al.*

1987), DSP56000 (Kloker 1986) from Motorola and ADSP-21xx (Roesgen 1986) families from Analog Devices. Today, we mention the TMS32Cx000 (x = 5 or 6) families of TI with VLIW architecture (*cf*. § 4.7), ADSP-219x and (Tiger) SHARC from Analog Devices or, in microcontroller version, 56F8xxxx from NXP.

Are DSPs obsolete? (Stewart *et al.* 1992). Depending on the bandwidth, current general-purpose microprocessors have sufficient performance. Specific applications will keep the DSP. Some components are called hybrids because they are difficult to classify, general-purpose microprocessor or DSP. This is the case with the Tricore from Siemens (Infineon Technologies AG), a 32-bit RISC microcontroller with electronics and instructions geared towards digital signal processing. Today, multicore microprocessors (hybrid approach) and SoCs (Systems-on-Chip, *cf*. § V1-1.2 and § V2-4.2.9) can integrate a specialized signal processing unit or a DSP to process flow multimedia. They offer an extension of the ISA (Instruction Set Architecture, *cf*. § V1-3.5) for multimedia applications (*cf*. § V4-2.7.1).

5.3. Microcontroller

A microcontroller, µC for short, is a conventional microprocessor with integrated I/O and random access and read-only memory functions, programmable or not, hence the designation of origin of Single-Chip microcomputer (SCC)[2]. The number of these functions and types of memory and their capacity are a compromise between the desired computing power, the functionalities and the cost (on this subject, *cf*. Cragon (1980)). The I/O functions are performed by parallel and serial controllers, timers and analog–digital and digital–analog converters. Serial interfaces are classic such as RS-232 (RS for Recommended Standard), I²C™ (Inter Integrated Circuit), SMB (System Management Bus), SPI™ (Serial Peripheral Interface), CAN (Controller Area Network) and VAN (Vehicle Area Network, *cf*. § V2-4.2.8). The time manager (timer) is a counter/timer with internal interruption. We find the same declination of data formats n manipulated only for a microprocessor (i.e. 4, 8, 16 and 32 bits). As for an MPU, the architectures are of the von Neumann or Harvard type (*cf*. § V1-3.2 and V1-3.4) and the instruction set can be of the CISC (Complex Instruction Set Computer) or RISC type. Since it integrates all the components of a small digital system into a single chip, it is very reliable. It can be seen as the precursor of SoC. Its field of use is the control of embedded systems. It is thus found in household appliances, cars, telephony, toys, etc.

Originally, the microcontroller families generally evolved in parallel with that of a generalist MPU, an example being the 68HC05 compared to the reference family

---

2 This acronym should not be confused with the "SCCC" (Single-Chip Cloud Computer) from the company Intel.

MC6800. There are often second sources. An example is the famous 8051, reference circuit of the MCS-51 family from Intel and also manufactured by companies like Atmel, Dallas, Philips or Siemens. Another is the Cortex M3 family from Arm®. Today, the microcontroller can be designed independently from a general-purpose reference microprocessor. Two examples are the AVR® and PIC® families of the companies Atmel and Microchip Technology[3].

The manufacturer declines the family while generally keeping the heart but it changes the characteristics of the circuits managing the inputs–outputs (i.e. variation of the configuration of the inputs–outputs). It can be the number of parallel, serial or time manager ports. The manufacturer can also offer different types of memory (RAM, ROM, EPROM (Erasable Programmable ROM (PROM)) or EEPROM for Electrically EPROM) with variable sizes but the capacity of the internal memories was at the beginning largely lower than that of a classic system where the memory is external. The 8751H, for example, had 4 KiB of EPROM. Two other examples were the MC68HC11P2 which has 32 KiB of ROM and 62 I/O lines and the MC68HC711L1 which has 16 KiB of EPROM, 512 bytes of EEPROM and 512 bytes of RAM. This obviously had repercussions on the encapsulation of the chip (number of external connections, quartz window due to the presence of an EPROM). Manufacturing technology also comes into play. The same microcontroller can be manufactured in CMOS (Complementary Metal–Oxide Semiconductor) or HMOS technology (High-density, High-performance or High-speed MOS, cf. § 2.4 of Darche (2004)), for reasons, for example, of electrical consumption. Other hardware options may be involved such as the fan-out of the output amplifiers. The characteristics offered are, as always, compromises between functionality and surface occupied on silicon. Table 5.1 gives the characteristics of the first emblematic components. Hyatt (1990) is the first patent concerning the microcontroller, subsequently invalidated because it has never been implemented (TI trial). The TMS 1000 (Boone and Cochran 1978) is classically designated as the first component. Let us also quote among the first the F3870/F3872 MK3870/MK3872/MK3876 compatible in terms of instructions with the F8 from Fairchild.

	References					
Characteristics	TMS 1000	8048	8051	MC6803	MC68HC11A0	MC68HC16Z1
Family	TMS 1000	MCS-48™	MCS-51™	MC6800	M68HC11	M68HC16
Manufacturer	TI	Intel	Intel	Motorola	Motorola	Motorola
Introductory year	1974	1976	1988	1978	1985	1998

3 It is they who bought the first in 2016.

Technology	PMOS[4]	NMOS[5]	HMOS	NMOS	HCMOS[6]	HCMOS
Number of transistors or technological generation	8000	LSI[7]	VLSI[8]	LSI	VLSI	VLSI
Package and number of pins	DIP[9] 28	DIP 40	DIP 40	DIP 40	PLCC[10] 52	QFP[11] 132/144
Initial internal clock frequency (MHz)	0.4	0.4	1	1	3	4,194
Architecture	Harvard	Harvard	Harvard	von Neumann	von Neumann	von Neumann
Data format (bit)	4	8	8	8	8	16
Width m of the external address bus (extended mode, bit)	-	10	16	16	16	20 + 4
External physical addressing capacity (bit)	0	1 Ki	64 Ki	64 Ki	64 Ki	1 Mi (program) and 1 Mi (data)
Internal RAM capacity (bit)	64×4	64×8	128×8	0 (MC6801 : 128×8)	256×8 (saved)	$1 Ki \times 8$ (saved)
Internal ROM capacity (bit)	$1 Ki \times 8$	$1 Ki \times 8$	$4 Ki \times 8$	$2 Ki \times 8$	0	0
Number of instructions	43	90	111	82	173	302
Number of addressing modes	3	5	8	6	6	10

4 For Positive (channel) MOS.

5 For Negative (channel) MOS.

6 For High-speed CMOS.

7 For Large-Scale Integration, cf.§ V1-1.2.

8 For Very LSI, cf. § V1-1.2.

9 For Dual-In-Line (DIL) Package.

10 For Plastic (J-) Leaded Chip Carrier.

11 For Quad Flat Package or FlatPak Package.

Number of registers	7	3	5	6	7	10 + 4 MAC
Number of interruptions (Reset not counted)		1	5	2	2	5
Parallel I/O port (format)	4 inputs (K) 8 outputs (O) 11 outputs (R)	27	32	29	22	48
Timer/event counter	0	8 bits	2 × 16	16 bits	16 bits	2 × 16
Hardware watchdog	No	No	No	No	Yes	Yes
Serial interface (type)	0	no	Yes	Yes	Yes (asynchronous and synchronous)	Yes (asynchronous and synchronous)
Test interface	No	No	No	No	No	Yes
Wired multiplication	No	No	Yes	Yes	Yes	Yes
Power supplies (V)	-15/+5	+5	+5	+5	+3-5	+2,7-3,6

Table 5.1. *Summary characteristics of the first generations of microcontrollers representative of the field*

The iconic 8048 of the MCS-48 family, and whose Figure 5.9 shows the simplified structure, was the first MCU (MicroController Unit) in 8-bit format.

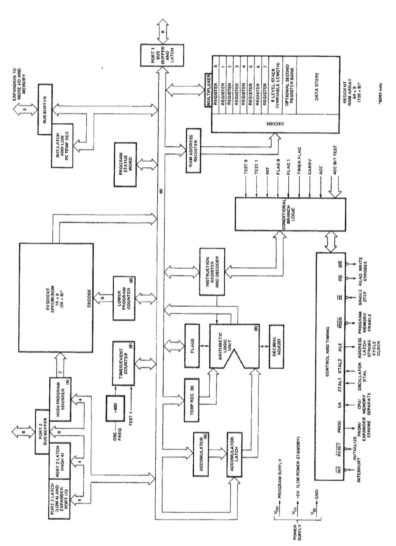

Figure 5.9. *Functional diagram of the 8048/8049 microcontrollers (Intel 1977, 1978)*

Modern MCUs (MicroController Unit) have A/D converters and, more rarely, D/A and time managers (timer), all three detailed in Chapter 3 of Darche (2003). The timer generally associated with a prescaler can count external or internal impulses coming from the clock. In particular, it allows you to implement Pulse Width Modulation (PWM), useful for servo control. Associated with the time manager, the watchdog or WDT for WatchDog Timer is essential for on-board applications. It allows you to recover the system during a hardware or software crash. The watchdog is a retriggerable (digital) monostable. Once armed, the program must periodically reset it (WDI signal for WatchDog Input in Figure 5.10). Otherwise, a signal will reset the µcontroller (Microcontroller) via a WDO (WatchDog Output) signal. This signal is activated when counting on a threshold stored in a register called OCR (Output Compare Register) or on an overflow. This functionality allows the software to start again on known bases in the event of an unexpected operation, even if it is up to the user to provide recovery procedures in order to return to the situation before crashing. It was presented in detail in § 3.3.1 of Darche (2003). The advanced version is the Time Processor Unit (TPU) capable of managing several channels. It is present, for example, in the MC68336/376 microcontroller.

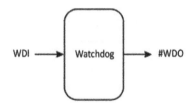

Figure 5.10. *Watch dog*

It can also integrate for specific application-specialized interfaces. Let us cite the Zero-Crossing Detector (ZCD) of an Alternating Current (AC) signal useful, for example, for noise-free load switching on the mains or the electronic amplifier (driver, *cf.* § 3.4.1 of Darche (2004)) specialized for LCD (Liquid Crystal Display) or high power switching (e.g. 68HC705V12 family). All these controllers process events with specialized interruptions based on the integrated elements (serial and parallel interfaces, timer).

Additional functions are offered such as external loading at boot, operation in standalone mode or in external bus and self-test functions. The boot-program loader function exists for MPUs (*cf.*, for example, the Transputer (*cf.* § 5.5) and the DSP TMS320C30). It is now widespread for microcontrollers. After initialization, a program called bootstrap is executed. Its function is to communicate via a communication interface, mostly serial, classic like SPI or debugging like JTAG in order to receive commands. These are used to program the flash-type read-only memory (FEEPROM for Flash EEPROM), more particularly in the BLS (Boot-Loader Section), or to write in random access memory and launch the application program thus loaded.

The microcontroller can operate in standalone mode without adding external components such as memory or an I/O controller. If necessary, extended bus operation is often offered. This memory expansion mechanism uses port lines as address, data and control lines (classic bus signals). The interface with these external components is generally "glueless", that is, it does not require additional external logic (on this subject, *cf.* § 1.2 of Darche (2003) and § 2.3). But that goes against the philosophy of this type of circuit which is to have "all-in-one". The advantages of a microcontroller are, however, lost and a version with MPU and conventional I/O circuits may be worth considering.

When the test mode is initialized, the microcontroller executes an internal program stored in internal ROM, distinct from that of the user, called "self-test". The role of this program is to check that the component is working properly. It therefore performs the control of internal registers, internal memory and peripheral circuits. For read-only memory, it is a question of carrying out a checksum (*cf.* § III.6.4 in Darche (2000)). For RAM, there is generally a write–read–check cycle of a binary pattern for each memory cell. For the input/output ports, one technique is the feedback of the input–outputs.

The memory is generally managed by bank in order to extend the storage space and to offer more flexibility for the designer. This means that the memory is subdivided into pages or bank (called prepare page for AMI S2000). One page address register contains the page number and another contains the movement within the page. The manufacturers of the first microcontrollers proposed an EPROM version to make the prototype and then be able to "ROMed"[12] the final application. The component case could have a quartz window to erase the memory. If not (economic version), we were talking about an OTP (One-Time Programmable) or OTPROM (One-Time EPROM) version. Special versions may contain a specialized ROM program. It can be, for example, a language interpreter as with the R65F11 and R65F12 of the Rockwell company which interpreted the Forth[13] language. The programmer had at his/her disposal the classic instructions of the MCS6502 and, in addition, 133 high-level instructions. Another example is Intel's 8051AH-BASIC (Beginner's All-purpose Symbolic Instruction Code). The

12 Technical jargon which refers to the fact of putting in read-only memory the final version of the application.
13 Rockwell Single-Chip Forth (RSC-Forth) more precisely.

interest is to be able to perform a complex calculation implemented in a HLL. A modern example (2018) is the pyboard module from MicroPython.org.

A microcontroller can have a hardware accelerator like a DSP; an example is the SH-DSP series from Hitachi. It will be described as "specialized", here in signal processing. Another example is the PIC32MZ incorporating a graphics controller.

5.4. Coprocessor

Running certain operations costs a lot of processor time such as evaluating an elementary floating-point function, a matrix calculation or a Fourier transform. The solution was to add an additional logical unit which would execute a specialized function more quickly in parallel. Three categories of processors assisting the microprocessor are to be considered according to their level of interaction with respect to the memory hierarchy (Birnbaum and Worley 1985, 1986). The SFU (Special Function Unit) interacts at the register level. It can be a specialized unit of calculation such as a multiplier or a encryption/decryption unit (*cf.* Helbig and Stringer (1977) for an example). The coprocessor represents the second category. It works on the cache. The last category interacts at the main memory level. Examples include the intelligent I/O processor or controller.

The ancestor of the coprocessor, the CoProcessor (CP), was one or more additional cards or modules like EAE (Extended Arithmetic Element) for the PDP (Programmable Data Processor) series of mini-computers from Digital Equipment Corporation (DEC). The purpose of this type of accelerator was to speed up the arithmetic operations of multiplication, division and logical shift for whole and fixed-point numbers and, subsequently, for floating-point numbers with, for example, the normalization operation (*cf.* § II.4.2.7.1 of Darche (2000)). Communication was generally done through registers.

Originally, a coprocessor is a processor with specialized function(s) that operates alongside the microprocessor in parallel. These functions are generally wired; their execution is very fast compared to their software version. We talk about mathematical coprocessor, FXU (Fixed-Point Unit), FPU (Floating-Point Unit, *cf.* § 5.4), graphic coprocessor or GPU (Graphics Processing Unit), generic I/O processor, etc. The term "co" describes the association of a specialized hardware accelerator with MPU and parallelism of execution. Initially external, these specialized units are now in most cases integrated.

A modern definition is that a coprocessor is a discrete component or an electronic sub-assembly integrated in a microprocessor that executes a particular class of instructions specialized in a field like graphics or mathematics. Its instruction set complements that of the microprocessor, which is a generalist. Thanks to its specialized architecture, it performs the requested operations more quickly. Thus, an 8087 accelerates calculations by a factor of 100 compared to an emulation using an 8086 instruction routine (Palmer *et al.* 1980). It works in parallel in a coordinated way with the microprocessor because it is not autonomous. It is a slave processing unit. The coprocessor because of its dependence on the MPU differs from independent processors such as, for example, the vector processor.

It has local memory in the form of registers. There is generally the same type of generic registers as an I/O controller (*cf.* Chapter 3 of Darche (2003)), i.e. data/control/status registers, as well as specialized registers or which facilitate error management. For the latter, an example is the pointer register on the last instruction and the operation code register of the last instruction executed from 8087[14]. These registers are compatible with the representations of the information handled or with the function. However, it does not have a Program Counter (PC) managed by the master processor. This local storage area is a characteristic distinction of the coprocessor compared to a specialized computing unit or SFU which is a kind of extension of the ALU (Birnbaum and Worley 1985, 1986).

The MPU is still on the initiative, taking responsibility for finding the instruction code. The instructions for the coprocessor are provided using the tracking technique (tracking instruction) or the distribution technique (dispatching instruction). With the first, the coprocessor listens to the bus and decodes the instruction flow in parallel. It only executes the instructions intended for it. Thus, the 8087 detected one of its instructions by the fact that it started with the binary pattern "11011", that is, the ASCII code (American Standard Code for Information Interchange, *cf.* § III.3.4 of Darche (2000)) escape (escape opcode). In this case, the instructions were seen as nop for the main processor. A defect is that it extends the instruction set of the microprocessor. We are talking about an I/O-oriented protocol. In the second, the launch is at the initiative of the MPU which sends the instruction to the coprocessor, thus avoiding a possible blocking of the system. Depending on its degree of autonomy, it can calculate the address of the operands and go get them. Its registers are projected in memory (memory mapping, *cf.* § 2.3 of Darche (2003) and § 2.1.1.1). We are talking about an interface projected in memory (memory-mapped interface). An example is the Weitek Abacus 3167 circuit which appears as a 64 KiB block of memory with the physical address starting at 0C0000000h. Its address space is projected into that of the MPU. Each address in this range has an instruction. By accessing a given address in the range considered, the MPU means a request to execute a specific instruction.

---

14 All of its records are detailed in Intel (2003, 2006).

Thus, the architecture of the coprocessor may be invisible to the MPU, partially or completely visible. In the first case, the MPU has no knowledge of its instruction set. This is the case for a circuit from a company other than that of the MPU. Partially visible means that the microprocessor recognizes its instruction set by an agreed binary pattern but does not decode the instruction. In the latter case, the MPU only transfers the code of the requested operation, the operands, the result and its status.

The interface between the two components can be synchronous or asynchronous. In the first case, the MPU awaits the end of the execution. In the second, the MPU continues to execute other instructions concurrently. On the other hand, it is necessary to carry out at least one synchronization to recover the result. Synchronization can be done using a busy signal like that of buses (*cf.* § V2-1.6) or by polling.

A coprocessor can have the functionality of raising an exception itself, for example, following a division by zero. If not, the MPU is warned as for I/O, either by a hardware interrupt request or by a polling policy (*cf.* § 4.2 of Darche (2003)), the MPU interrogating it periodically or not.

The math coprocessor was first an external component independent of any family of MPUs. As first reference having the function of multiplier/divider, there were circuits 74S508 and 74S516 (TTL family for Transistor–Transistor Logic, *cf.* § 2.3.2 of Darche (2004)). The first complex components include the APU (Arithmetic Processing Unit) Am9511a and the FPP (Floating-Point Processor) Am9512 from AMD. Another acronym was NCU for Number Cruncher Unit, the name of the company National Semiconductor (NS) for its circuit MM57109 in the PMOS technology. Dedicated to a microprocessor, we can mention the Weitek 1067 circuits for the 286 and 1167 for the 386. At Intel, these are the 8087, 80287 and 80387 and, for Motorola, the MC68881. Integrated Devices Technology, Inc. used the term FPA for Floating-Point Accelerator core. Let us quote the R2010 and R3010 which were associated with MIPS microprocessors of the RISC architecture. The mathematical processors available today industrially respect the standardized formats of the ANSI/IEEE Std 754-1985 (IEEE 1985) standards, in floating point and in BCD (Binary Coded Decimal).

The graphics coprocessor is part of the display interface (*cf.* § 5.1 of Darche (2003)). Its ancestor was the VDC (Video Display Coprocessor) which was responsible for generating the management signals of the display device, at the time a CRT screen (CRT cathode, *cf.* § 6.2.1 of Darche (2003)). The GPU performs complex image calculations such as rendering. Its command processor (CP) receives its commands via specialized registers projected in memory (memory-mapped I/O register, *cf.* § 2.3 of Darche (2003)) or a queue implemented in the main memory. For economic reasons, the GPU can also be integrated into the chipset (IGP for Integrated Graphics Processor). AMD recently (2011) launched a microprocessor that merges processor and GPU on the same chip via unified memory under the name of APU for Accelerated Processing Unit. Today, thanks to its power, like the MPU, it has become programmable. The concept of coprocessor is therefore evolving. We then speak of GPGPU (General-Purpose (computing on) GPU) and cGPU (computational GPU).

Another example of a coprocessor is the I/O processor which processes information alone (in a single processor environment) using functions dedicated to the application domain. Let us quote as example the generic I/O processor (IOP), also called the front-end processor such as the 8089 (El-Ayat 1979) of the company Intel which executes independent programs by playing the role of an "intelligent" DMA (Direct Memory Access) controller. Its ancestor was the AP-120B (Floating Point Systems 1979) which was a machine providing the function of a mathematical processor attached to a conventional mini, central or super computer.

The main drawback is that it is an additional component or logic unit which occupies a certain area of the printed circuit or chip and which therefore adds current consumption and therefore additional energy dissipation.

In summary, the coprocessor originally executed an instruction in parallel (example of the mathematical coprocessor). It has evolved towards the execution of fixed functions (example of the GPU). Modern versions execute a program in parallel (example of the GPGPU). It can have a private memory (display memory, for example, for a GPU) and it shares the main memory.

5.5. Parallelism processors

In the 1960s, Research became interested in computers with parallel computing capacity. A family of microprocessors appeared at the end of the 1980s, the transputer[15] from the company INMOS, mounted in particular on a module called TRAM (TRAnsputer Module, Figure 5.11(a)) which allowed with its four high-speed[16] bidirectional serial links [3:0] (5, 10 and 20 Mb/s) to design a parallel machine at a lower cost in the form of a grid of communicating T processors (Figure 5.11(b)), or even a torus by back looping the links at the ends.

---

15 Contraction of the transistor and computer names.

16 For the era!

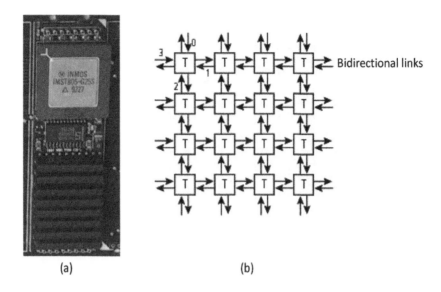

(a)   (b)

Figure 5.11. *Example of TRAM and grid of T transputers. For a color version of this figure, see www.iste.co.uk/darche/microprocessor3.zip*

The idea of links has been taken up by certain manufacturers such as TI for its DSP TMS320C40 (six communication ports) and Analog Devices with the ADSP-21060 (six links) from the SHARC family. It is also found in the IEEE 1355–1995 standard (IEEE 1995, 2000).

5.6. Conclusion

This chapter has presented specific cases of microprocessors. These were bit-slice processors, digital signal processors, microcontroller and coprocessor and, finally, components specialized in parallel computing.

Datasheet

In general, manufacturers share technical information in two documents, the characteristic sheet or datasheet (*cf.* § 3.2 of Darche (2004)) and the document describing the architecture and software operation. The datasheet is destined for the electronics technician and gives the electrical, time and mechanical specifications of the component. It also describes the function of each pin and gives functional information. The list of instructions and their coding is present. Today, the documentation containing the software developer's manual in Intel 64 and IA-32 architecture (IA for Intel Architecture) is gathered in eight volumes for a total of almost 5,000 pages!

6.1. Electrical specifications

We must distinguish electrical specifications pertaining to logic signals from those pertaining to electrical power supply. For the former, they were described in § 3.3 of Darche (2004), supplemented by § 3.4 of Darche (2012). They depend on the microelectronic logic chosen.

6.1.1. *Supply voltage*

The supply voltage of the microprocessors is also linked to the manufacturing technology used (Figure V1-1.15). PMOS (Positive (channel) Metal–Oxide Semiconductor (MOS)) technology required a double power supply (-15 V and +5 V). With NMOS (Negative (channel) MOS) technology, it has switched to single voltage (single power supply voltage), for example, the classic +5 V. CMOS (Complementary MOS) allows a wide power range. Figure 6.1 shows the evolution over time of the supply voltage of the MPU (MicroProcessor Unit). First in steps at +12 V, +5 V and +3.3 V, the voltage then decreased linearly below the single volt after 2010.

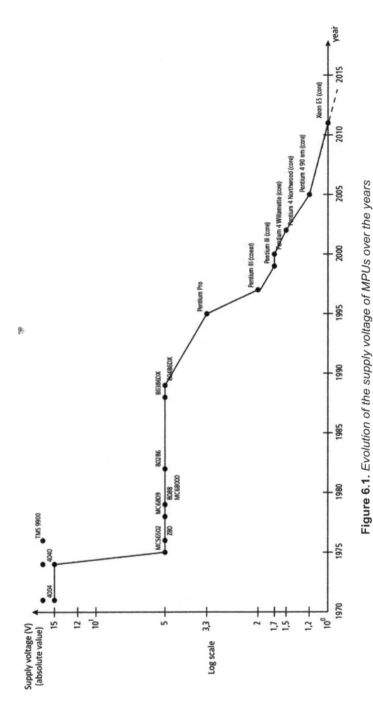

Figure 6.1. *Evolution of the supply voltage of MPUs over the years*

6.1.2. *Power consumption*

We must distinguish between the average consumption and peak consumption. The i486 microprocessor passed the single ampere mark in 1990. Today's microprocessors (2015) exceed 30 A at peak at 3 GHz (Travers 2015). Another example is a third-generation Intel Core family MPU that can consume 112 A with 77 W TDP (Thermal Design Power) (Intel 2013). Also, the component has many power pins. The Intel® Core ™ i7 MPU in an LGA 1155 package (Land Grid Array), for example, has 286 power pins and 529 ground pins. To this must be added one to several tens of peripheral decoupling capacitors.

The dissipated power is linked to the power density (W/cm^2) of the chip and to the heat dissipation properties of the package and, if the latter is equipped, of its heat sink. In the CMOS technology, the total power breaks down into several terms:

$$P_{total} = P_{dynamic} + P_{static} + P_{leakage} + P_{shortcircuit} \qquad [6.1]$$

To simplify, we are only interested in the first two. Static power P_{static} is related to the sum of the leakage currents I_{CC} due mainly to the parasitic diodes. It is given by the following formula:

$$P_{static} = V_{CC} \times I_{CC} \qquad [6.2]$$

The dynamic power $P_{dynamic}$ is linked to the activity of the component. It is broken down (formula [6.3]) into a dissipated transient power P_T due to the capacitance inherent in this technology (switching current) and to the transient currents linked to switching, that is, short circuit (through current) and a dissipated load power P_L due to capacitive loads (capacitive-load power). TI (1997) details the calculations. It is given by the following formula:

$$P_{dynamic} = P_T + P_L \qquad [6.3]$$

We must therefore consider the number of switching logic levels by introducing a switching activity factor α, generally equal to 1 or 0.5. This gives the following simplified formula with the supply voltage V_{CC}, the sum of the parasitic capacitances C_{tot} and the switching frequency f:

$$P_{dynamic} = \alpha \times V_{CC}^2 \times C_{tot} \times f \qquad [6.4]$$

We see that power dissipation varies quadratically depending on the supply voltage V, which justifies the drop in the supply voltage of MPU cores which today revolves around the volt (*cf.* exercise 6.1). Currently, it is less than 1 V, the limit being the threshold voltage V_{th} for a Field Effect Transistor (FET). For a given dissipated power, lowering the supply voltage increases the clocking frequency. The first industrial microprocessor to pass the GHz mark (1.1 GHz to be exact) was PowerPC from IBM (Silberman *et al.* 1998a, 1998b) with a voltage of 1.8 V. It also varies according to the capacity total interference C of the transistors and the links of the chip and as a function of the clocking frequency f. The transition to a lower technological node decreases C because the size of the transistors decreases but the number of transistors increases. The frequency caps approximately 4 GHz because of the energy wall (*cf.* § V1-1.5).

6.1.3. *Power supply profiles*

To reduce their electrical consumption, modern microprocessors and Programmable Logic Circuits (PLD for Programmable Logic Device, *cf.* Chapter 4 of Darche (2004)) and, more generally, high-density logic circuits are supplied with several voltages dependent on microelectronic technologies, which requires a power supply with several rails. As a classic example, the I/O interfaces are at 5 or 3.3 V, while the core of the MPU is at a voltage close to 1 V. There can be up to five to seven different voltages. Like the clock with its different clock domains or CDC (Clock Domain Crossing, *cf.* § 2.4), we then speak of power domains. The consequence is a risk of failure by latch-up effect (*cf.* § 3.5.1 of Darche (2004)), that is, an unwanted current flow, essentially during power-up (turn-on or power-on) or shutdown (turn-off or power-off), which can intervene if a voltage is missing or disappears. Another scenario is the powering of several logic systems connected to a bus (system-level bus contention). To avoid this, it is necessary to sequence the application of the different power supplies. Figure 6.2 shows the different possible profiles. In (a), it is about sequential sequencing. Core voltage must be applied before the I/O voltage. This second one is applied only when the core voltage has reached a V_{OK} threshold, in general the regulation value or after a fixed delay. The application of the second voltage appears after a time Δt. Note that certain circuits require a reverse order (case of the circuit MPC8260 (HiP3) of the company Freescale Semiconductor), as illustrated in Figure 6.2(a).

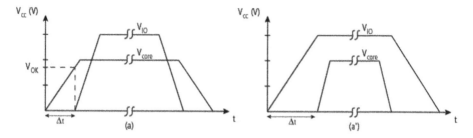

Figure 6.2. *Power profiles for complex logic components*

Profile b (Figure 6.3) is called "ratiometric sequencing", that is, proportional sequencing. The two power supplies grow at the same time but with different speeds to reach the regulation value at the same time. The supply voltage difference ΔV increases. A major shortcoming of this approach is that the component may not withstand too high an instantaneous voltage difference before regulation. But to avoid, during the power-up phase, a bus containment problem (*cf.* § V2-1.1), that is, a low impedance state of the output buffers, the profile (b') must be observed. Thus, the I/O buffers will not disturb the operation of the bus and will provide valid data before the logic system connects to a bus.

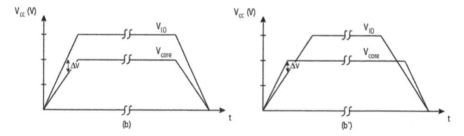

Figure 6.3. *Ratiometric power profiles*

The last profile (Figure 6.4), simultaneous power, having identical (de) growth rates, seems to be the classic solution because it is simple to implement. Before regulation, the differences in voltage ΔV and time Δt are zero.

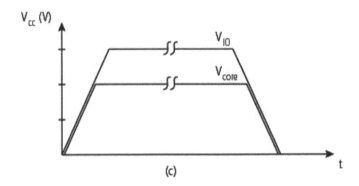

Figure 6.4. *Simultaneous power profile*

6.1.4. *Energy savings*

Energy consumption and dissipation translate into a high energy cost (consumption of electronics and cooling) for a supercomputer and a data center. For a mobile device, this translates into a reduced autonomy of use and space constraints which imply constraints on the size of the battery and the packages and the number of components. To save energy, it is mainly necessary to intervene on the activity of the logical subsets and their power supplies.

Knowing that a logic gate in the CMOS technology consumes almost no current at rest, the main clock is sometimes put at rest (i.e. more oscillation) or the clock signals of one or more logical subsets of the system are blocked, for example, by an AND logic gate (clock gating). Thus, the dynamic part of power dissipation P_D becomes almost zero. The designer of synchronous systems must take this functionality into account. In particular, a static core is favorable rather than its dynamic version so as not to lose data. This type of core allows the frequency to be lowered to 0 Hz (i.e. stopped) for almost zero consumption. An example of a static core is the CDP1802 (*cf.* Table 4.2(b)) used, for example, in the Galileo space probe (Russell 1992) and the 65C02 respectively from the companies RCA and Western Digital Center (WDC). The clock can also be slowed down.

For the power supply, this same blocking technique can be used to save energy, the power supply for power supply areas or logic sub-assemblies can be stopped. The technique is called power gating with the problems of the aforementioned power and power-on domains.

More flexible, several Power Management Modes (PMMs) are implemented. Let us cite the stop and standby (idle) modes. The first stops the oscillation. The oscillator is restarted by an external reset signal or by an interrupt request, which consumes less energy than the first method. Depending on the structure of the oscillator, the restart is not immediate. For a quartz model, there is a non-negligible dead time of the order of 10 ms during which the signal is not within the nominal voltage and frequency characteristics. This time is to be taken into account in the power balance. A ring oscillator cancels this time. The standby mode preserves the operation of the oscillator, time bases (timer) and, possibly, a Real-Time Clock (RTC, *cf.* § 3.3.2 of Darche (2003)) but stops the MPU. These time bases are used to periodically start up the MPU.

There is an open industry specification for modern systems called ACPI for Advanced Configuration and Power Interface originally developed in the mid-1990s by the companies Intel, Microsoft, Phoenix and Toshiba. It offers a hierarchy of MPU energy management states. At the top of the latter, there are five global states of the system G[3:0] and S4, five global states of the device (device power state) D[3:0], four states of sleep (sleeping and soft-off state) S[5:0] and device performance processor states P[n:0] (n ≤ 255). A P-state for Performance state P_i is a couple (frequency, voltage) given when the processor executes instructions (power saving state). The value i = 0 is the highest frequency. A C-state (proCessor state) concerns the processor when it is idle (i.e. no execution, idle power saving state) with the exception of C0 which is the operating state. C1 is the halt state where no instruction is executed but where it can return to the previous mode without delay. C2 is the mode where the clock is stopped (stop-clock state). The internal state is preserved but the restart is longer. C3 is the sleep mode. The consistency of the caches is not preserved. Other states can be defined (up to C8). Thus, the Haswell architecture defines up to 11 states (C0-10). It is also necessary to distinguish according to the architectures: the Core C-states (CC-states), Package C-states (PC-states) and Logical C-states (LC-states). Finally, we must mention the throttling states T-state[1] T_i which controls the clock cycles (clock gating) in %, i = 0 corresponding to 100% of clock cycles (normal operation) without change to either the supply voltage or the clock frequency, unlike P_i. T_i states, which are now obsolete, have been introduced to limit heat dissipation. All these types can be managed in particular in the BIOS (Basic Input/Output System, *cf.* § V5-3.5.3 and Chapter 4 of Darche (2003)) by the setup program. Figure 6.5 summarizes the different states of a latest generation Intel processor (2018).

---

1 This term should not be confused with the T-state of the base clock period (*cf.* § 2.4.1).

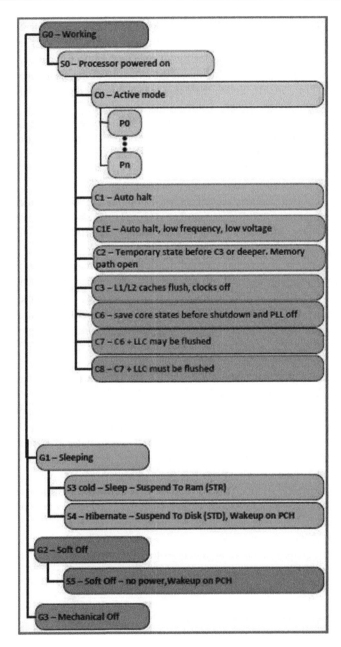

Figure 6.5. *MPU power states (Intel 2018). For a color version of this figure, see www.iste.co.uk/darche/microprocessor3.zip*

Figure 6.6 shows the increase in the energy efficiency of microcontrollers or MCUs (MicroController Unit) since 2000 to meet a demand from manufacturers of mobile systems.

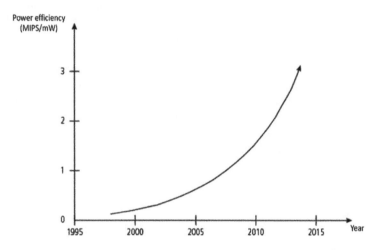

Figure 6.6. *Temporal evolution of the power efficiency of microcontrollers (from IEEE (2015))*

6.1.5. *Peripheral components*

Each component in a digital system generates unwanted electrical effects due to parasitic components such as an inductor, a capacitor or a parasitic resistor (Figure 6.7). The power supply of integrated circuits was discussed in § 3.6.7 of Darche (2012).

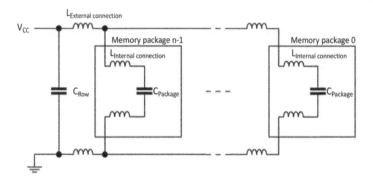

Figure 6.7. *Electrical modeling of the power supply of logic integrated circuit packages (Darche 2012)*

6.2. Processor hardware initialization

The microprocessor, when powered up, is in an undetermined state. When the supply voltage has become stable and it is within a range permitted by the electrical characteristics, it is necessary to initialize the microprocessor so that its state is known. This initialization is done by a time-calibrated pulse applied to a dedicated microprocessor pin (ReSeT or RST) which triggers the execution of the associated initialization routine, the latter being of the interrupt type (*cf.* Chapter V4-5). This signal is active in a state. As long as it is kept active, the component remains in an initialization state defined at design time. Figure 6.8 shows an elementary initialization circuit composed of an RC network (Resistor–Capacitor), the push button BP and a signal shaping gate of the "Schmitt trigger" type (Schmitt 1938). § V4-5.2.2 presents the software aspect of initialization.

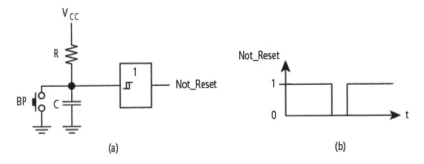

Figure 6.8. *Initialization RC network*

There are several forms of initialization. The first brings together the manual and power-up resets or POR for Power-On Reset, both of which share the external Reset input. The second is the Reset of good functioning or COP (Computer Operating Properly) which is associated with a routine of management of a watchdog (WDT or COP Timer, *cf.* § 3.3.1 of Darche (2003)). The last one is related to the monitoring of proprioceptive parameters of the system like the voltages and the frequency of clocks (voltage and clock monitor Reset). In conventional computer systems, a distinction must be made between cold initialization (hard/cold reset) and warm initialization (software/warm reset). The first is done when the system has just started. The second is generally a connection to a part of the management routine of the first. Reset is a hardware initialization which cannot be prevented (we will say "hidden"). It should be noted that some coprocessors and I/O controllers do not have an initialization signal but a register which, when accessed or written, initiates the initialization of the component. An example is the MC6850 asynchronous serial interface controller from Motorola.

Certain logical subsets may not be initialized, such as test and debug logic (BIST for Built-In Self-Test, *cf.* § V5-2.3) during a Reset. Some components have more than one power signal, such as the Pentium. Thus, its second signal called INIT, active alone (on the front), saves the content of its data and instruction caches. But its combination with Reset allows initializing the BIST sequence. The INIT signal is seen and recognized by the processor as a conventional interrupt.

In summary, today's initialization circuit is complex. It is associated with the watchdog (*cf.* § 5.3), the supervisor (SVS for Supply Voltage Supervisor) and the supply voltage sequencer.

6.3. Mechanical, electrical and thermal aspects of the package

The mechanical aspect essentially concerns the packaging of the electronic chip. Early microprocessors used discrete logic packaging technology. The latter was described exhaustively in § 3.3 of Darche (2004) and 3.7 of Darche (2012). Today, three types of packages are mainly used for powerful microprocessors, the BGA (Ball Grid Array) and the LGA (Land Grid Array) that Figure 6.9 presents and which replaced the PGA (Pin Grid Array). Clear or coded marking references the component. Note the presence of discrete passive components below the package, in these case capacitors, for power supply decoupling.

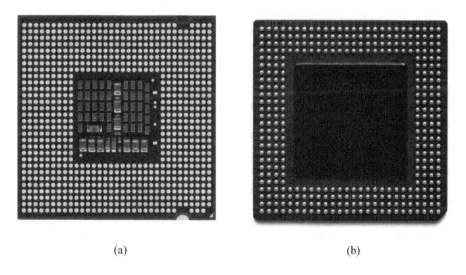

(a)   (b)

Figure 6.9. *Bottom view of LGA packages (a) of a Core 2 Quad Q6600 and BGA (b) of a Pentium MMX from Intel. For a color version of this figure, see www.iste.co.uk/darche/microprocessor3.zip*

A connection (pad, lead, ball or pin) at the level of the package is modeled electrically by a choke (i.e. an inductor) in series and a serial RC network in parallel as shown in Figure 6.10. These parasitic components are responsible for the electrical and temporal modifications of the electrical signal. Between pins, parasitic capacities will also exist. With high frequency (i.e. higher than MHz) of the signals, inductive and capacitive couplings will induce noise in these signals.

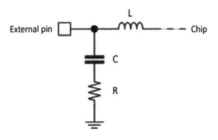

Figure 6.10. *Simplified equivalent electrical circuit of a pin (Figure 3.64 of Darche (2012))*

An electronic chip can be mounted on a printed circuit without a package. This technology is called COB for Chip On Board. The welded chip is protected by a resin coating. The interest lies in a gain in surface area, a lower packaging cost and better control of the impedance of the connections compared to the classical solution of the package. Vibration resistance is also improved. The solution taken to the extreme is the embedded memory (this will be covered in a future book by the author on memories) in a SoC (System-on-Chip).

The package is a protection against external attacks of an electrical, mechanical, chemical nature, etc. It can thus serve in its metallic version, as an electro-magnetic shield (shielding). Another major role is caloric dissipation. Its thermal resistance (unit: °C/W) must be as low as possible in order to be able to evacuate the calories released by the electronic chip whose internal temperature T_j (chip-junction temperature) must not exceed a threshold $T_{j,\ max}$ which varies from 80 to 105°C depending on the processor. Ceramic and metal (copper, aluminum and iron with increasing thermal resistance value) are excellent thermal conductors, unlike molded plastic. Modern MPU packages are equipped with a heat diffuser or IHS (Integrated Heat Spreader), usually made of metal, which allows the heat to be dissipated from the chip (die) by offering a larger surface. The thermal connection between the chip and this spreader is made by thermal paste. The spreader can be glued or welded. The superior solution is to use a heat sink mounted on it and the printed circuit can participate in this cooling. Forced circulation of a heat transfer fluid, using a pump, may be the last solution, air, using a "cooler", or a liquid, water or nitrogen, for example.

A package with a high number of connections increases the overall cost of the encapsulation. This high number depends on the year considered. In 1970, 40 pins was a high number for a DIP type package (Dual-In-Line Package, *cf.* § 3.3 of Darche (2004)). At the end of 2011, there were more than 2000 connections with, for example, the LGA 2011 (2011 contacts). Today (2016–2018), the number of pins is rising above 2000 with the LGA 2066 and 3647. Recall that more than half of the pins of a modern MPU are intended for the power supplies of the component (*cf.* § 6.1.2). When the number of pins was limited, multiplexing of the signals was necessary, first those of different buses, for example, the data with the addresses, then those of the same bus, for example, the bits of high address with those of low address. Coding of certain signals can also be envisaged with an external decoding in order to be able to use them.

6.4. Conclusion

This chapter was devoted to the technical specification sheet (datasheet) of a microprocessor and, more specifically, the electrical component.

Conclusion of Volume 3

The microprocessor is at the heart of current digital systems. A component having existed for 50 years, it has sounded the death knell for many computer classes (the famous expression killer micro, *cf.* § V1-1.2). Due to its technical heritage, this programmable logic component sequentially executes the instructions of a program stored in main memory (i.e. primary). It basically consists of a whole number Processing Unit (PU) controlled by a Control Unit (CU) and a set of registers for storing its internal state.

This third volume was mainly devoted to the material aspects of this component. After the basic definitions and history, the interface of this component was presented. The functionalities of its various internal sub-assemblies have been described. A generational classification has been proposed with representative industrial examples. This chapter ended with the description of its characteristic sheet which brings together its temporal, electrical, mechanical and thermal characteristics.

The hardware design of this component requires the expertise of multiple fields ranging from microelectronic technology to functional architecture through logic and the design of logic circuits. It is obviously in close relation with software design. Optimization criteria will be considered for cost, power consumption, performance and areas of application. Each aspect of functionality corresponds to a silicon surface, and functional compromises must be made.

Today (i.e. from 2000), the issue of energy savings has consequences for the design of conventional microprocessors (i.e. for general use) and, above all, that of specialized models intended, for example, for embedded applications but not for the same reasons. The former, which are used in data centers called server farms, represent 2% of the total world energy consumed and must limit their carbon footprint. The latter are embedded in mobile systems and must be optimized to consume as little current as possible to increase the autonomy of use.

The next volume, logical continuation of this book, is concerned with the software aspect. This covers the coding and format of the instructions, the addressing modes, the instruction set, as well as complementary concepts such as alignment, orthogonality and execution modes.

NOTE.– The concepts discussed in this book will be completed later on compared to the new ones introduced. The second volume will focus on the modern aspects of processors from the 1980s and 1990s, in particular virtual memory and Instruction-Level Parallelism (ILP). The third volume will focus on multicore parallelism and security.

Exercises

Here are some exercises that complement the concepts presented in this book. Their numbering refers to the chapter with which they are associated.

Chapter 2 exercises

E2.1. A non-multiplexed bus of address A[15:0] of the MC6809. Determine its addressing capacity.

Answer. The bus therefore has 16 address wires (width m = 16 bits). Its addressing capacity will be $C = 2^{16}$ words or 65,536 (= 64 Ki) memory words. As it is an 8-bit format processor which therefore handles data in this format, its addressing capacity is therefore 64 KiB.

Chapter 3 exercises

E3.1. Study an Arithmetic and Logic Unit (ALU) in n = 2-bit format which performs the addition or a basic logic operation (i.e. AND, OR or NOT functions) on external command.

Answer. Figure E3.33 shows the flow diagram of such a subset.

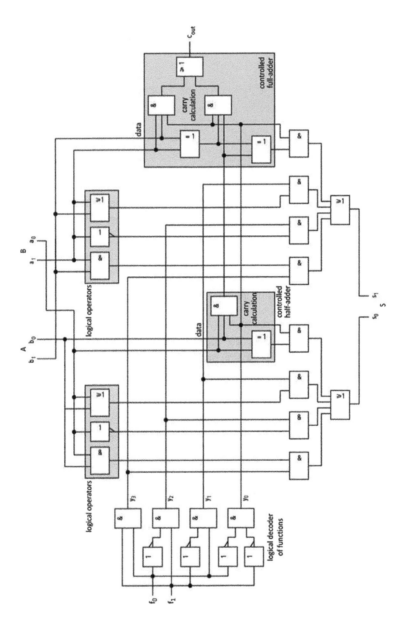

Figure E3.33. *Basic ALU (format n = 2 bits)*

The truth table of the command is given in Table E3.4.

Orders		
f_1	f_0	**Digital or logical functions**
0	0	addition
0	1	OR
1	0	NOT
1	1	AND

Table E3.4. *UAL command truth table*

E3.2. Study the incrementer of an address A in n = 3 bits format.

Answer. The system's Input/Output (I/O) must first be described (Figure E3.34). A carry c_{out} makes it possible to detect a possible overshooting of format and therefore a return to the initial value 0 (modulo 2^n calculation).

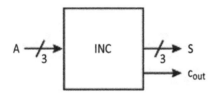

Figure E3.34. *Black box of the incrementer*

Table E3.5 gives the calculation table of the incrementer, which is also its truth table that describes the operation of this system.

Input A			Output S		
a_2	a_1	a_0	s_2	s_1	s_0
0	0	0	0	0	1
0	0	1	0	1	0
0	1	0	0	1	1
0	1	1	1	0	0
1	0	0	1	0	1
1	0	1	1	1	0
1	1	0	1	1	1
1	1	1	0	0	0

Table E3.5. *Calculation/truth table of the incrementer*

This gives the following Boolean equations:

$$s_0 = \bar{a}_0$$

$$s_1 = \bar{a}_1 a_0 + a_1 \bar{a}_0 = a_1 \oplus a_0$$

$$s_2 = \bar{a}_2 a_1 a_0 + a_2(\bar{a}_1 + \bar{a}_0) = \bar{a}_2(a_1 a_0) + a_2(\overline{a_1 \cdot a_0}) = a_2 \oplus (a_1 a_0)$$

The carry output c_{out} for the upper row allows possible cascade rise. Its logical equation is:

$$c_{out} = a_2 a_1 a_0$$

Figure E3.35 shows the corresponding flow diagram.

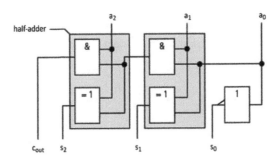

Figure E3.35. *Incrementer in n = 3-bit format*

E3.3. Study the decrementer of an address A in the format n = 3 bits.

Answer. First you have to define your I/O (Figure E3.36).

Figure E3.36. *Black box of the decrementer*

Table E3.6 gives the calculation table of the incrementer, which is also its truth table that describes the operation of this system.

Input A			Output S		
a_2	a_1	a_0	s_2	s_1	s_0
0	0	0	1	1	1
0	0	1	0	0	0
0	1	0	0	0	1
0	1	1	0	1	0
1	0	0	0	1	1
1	0	1	1	0	0
1	1	0	1	0	1
1	1	1	1	1	0

Table E3.6. *Truth table of the decrementer*

The truth table of the decrementer is:

$$s_0 = \bar{a}_0$$

$$s_1 = \bar{a}_1\bar{a}_0 + a_1a_0 = \overline{a_1 \oplus a_0}$$

$$s_2 = a_2a_1 + a_2a_0 + \bar{a}_2\bar{a}_1a_0 = a_2(a_1 + a_0) + \bar{a}_2\bar{a}_1a_0$$

Figure E3.37 shows the corresponding flow diagram.

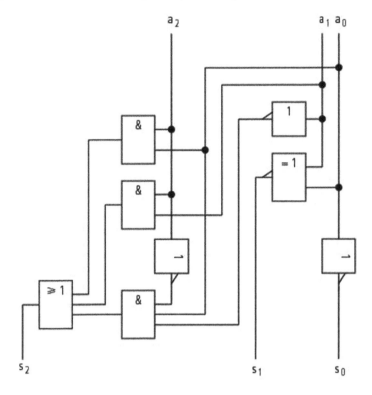

Figure E3.37. *Decrementer in n = 3-bit format*

E3.4. Give the logical equation of the sign indicator S for the 2^n's complement representation of the microcontrollers of the AVR family of the company Atmel from the classic flags N and V. Interpret it.

Answer

$$S = N \oplus V$$

When two numbers are added and there is an overflow, the sign changes. The S indicator gives the real sign of the result even if it is false. This means that $S = N$ if $V = 0$ and $S = \overline{N}$ if $V = 1$. The exclusive OR is here seen as a controlled inverter (*cf.* § 2.2.10 of Darche (2002)).

E3.5. Study a right barrel shifter in n = 4-bit format designed with four-input multiplexers (MUX).

Answer. A barrel shifter is a logical system that allows each input to be linked to any output according to a selection word. Each MUX allows you to select one of the address bits. Figure E3.38 shows the corresponding flow diagram.

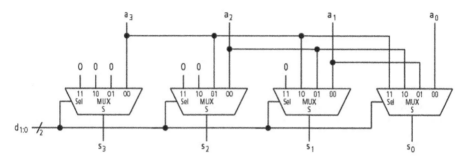

Figure E3.38. *Right shift in n = 4-bit format based on 4:1 multiplexers*

E3.6. Study a left barrel shifter in n = 8-bit format designed with multiplexers (MUX) with two inputs.

Answer. Each MUX selects the bit of the upper story, either of the same row or one of the rows to the right of its position. Figure E3.39 shows the corresponding flow diagram.

E3.7. Give the definition of a register.

Answer. A register is a short-term memory with a capacity of a word in format n and which operates at the speed of the component that hosts it (i.e. that integrates it). Its access therefore does not slow down the latter.

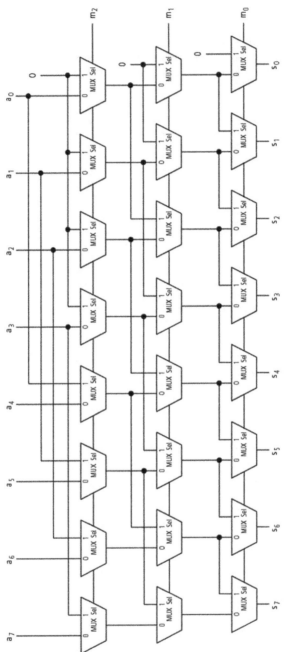

Figure E3.39. *Logarithmic shifter (n = 8-bit format)*

Chapter 6 exercises

E6.1. What is the gain in power consumed by passing the voltage of the external logic from $V_1 = 5$ V to $V_2 = 3.3$ V?

Answer. We must distinguish between dynamic and static powers. We know from [6.4] that the dynamic power P_D is equal to:

$$P_D = \alpha \times V_{CC}^2 \times C_{tot} \times f \times (1 - \delta)$$

The ratio δ of the two powers gives:

$$\delta = 1 - \frac{V_1^2}{V_2^2} \qquad\qquad\qquad [E6.5]$$

This gives a gain δ of 57% in dynamics. Recall that the static power P_S [6.2] is equal to:

$$P_S = V_{CC} \times I_{CC}$$

With the same reasoning as before, this gives a gain δ of 33%.

Appendices

Instruction Description Examples

The two appendices are examples of instruction descriptions. Note that the field describing the state of the flags includes the Boolean expressions that calculate it. In addition, the encoding of the instructions is sometimes omitted.

Appendix 1

AVR Instruction Set

OR – Logical OR

Description:

Performs the logical OR between the contents of register Rd and register Rr and places the result in the destination register Rd.

Operation:

(i)   Rd ← Rd v Rr

	Syntax:	Operands:	Program Counter:
(i)	OR Rd,Rr	$0 \le d \le 31, 0 \le r \le 31$	PC ← PC + 1

16-bit Opcode:

0010	10rd	dddd	rrrr

Status Register (SREG) and Boolean Formula:

I	T	H	S	V	N	Z	C
–	–	–	⇔	0	⇔	⇔	–

S: N ⊕ V. For signed tests.

V: 0
      Cleared

N: R7
      Set if MSB of the result is set; cleared otherwise.

Z: R̄7• R̄6 •R̄5• R̄4• R̄3 •R̄2• R̄1• R̄0
      Set if the result is $00; cleared otherwise.

R (Result) equals Rd after the operation.

Example:

```
        or    r15,r16    ; Do bitwise or between registers
        bst   r15,6      ; Store bit 6 of r15 in T Flag
        brts  ok         ; Branch if T Flag set
        ...
ok:     nop              ; Branch destination (do nothing)
```

Words: 1 (2 bytes)
Cycles: 1

Figure A.1. *Example of instructional documentation –
architecture of AVR microcontrollers from Atmel*

Appendix 2

intel   THE 8086/8088 ARCHITECTURE AND INSTRUCTIONS

AAA — ASCII ADJUST FOR ADDITION

Operation

if ((AL) & 0FH) > 9 or (AF) = 1 then
   (AL) ← (AL) + 6
   (AH) ← (AH) + 1
   (AF) ← 1
(CF) ← (AF)
(AL) ← (AL) & 0FH

Flags Affected

AF, CF
OF, PF, XF, ZF undefined

Description

AA (ASCII Adjust for Addition) changes the contents of register AL to a valid unpacked decimal number; the high-order half-byte is zeroed. AAA updates AF and CF; the content of OF, PF, SF and ZF is undefined following execution of AAA.

Encoding

0 0 1 1 0 1 1 1

AAA Operands	Clocks	Transfers	Bytes	AAA Coding Example
(no operands)	8	—	1	AAA

Figure A.2. *Example of instructional documentation for MPU 8086 (Intel 89)*

Acronyms

This section includes all of the acronyms used in this volume. They will be introduced once per chapter.

General

A

A	Address
AC	Alignment Check
AC	Alternating Current
AC	Auxiliary Carry (status) flag (i.e. AF, DC and H)
ACC or AC	Accumulator register
Ack	Acknowledgment
ACPI	Advanced Configuration and Power Interface
ACU	Address Computation Unit, synonyms: AGU, DAG
AD	Address/Data
A/D	Analog/Digital
ADC	Analog-to-Digital Converter
AF	Auxiliary carry (status) Flag (i.e. AC, DC and H)
AGP	Accelerated Graphics Port
AGU	Address Generation Unit (DSP), synonyms: ACU, DAG

AL	ALways (unconditional)
AL	Assembly Language
ALU	Arithmetic and Logic Unit
APU	Accelerated Processing Unit
APU	Arithmetic Processing Unit
AS	Address Space
AS	Address Strobe
ASCII	American Standard Code for Information Interchange
ASIP	Application-Specific Instruction set Processor
ASL	Arithmetic Shift Left
ASP	Application-Specific Processor
ASR	Arithmetic Shift Right
AT	Advanced Technology
ATA	AT Attachment
AXP	Almost eXactly PRISM

B

b	bit (i.e. BIT)
B	Break (flag)/FPU Busy (x87)
B	Byte
BASIC	Beginner's All-purpose Symbolic Instruction Code
BCD	Binary Coded Decimal
BCLK	Bus CLocK (Intel)
BGA	Ball Grid Array
BHE	Bus High Enable (Intel 8086)
BIOS	Basic Input/Output System
BIST	Built-In Self-Test
BIT	BInary digiT or Binary digIT

BIU	Bus Interface Unit
BLS	Boot-Loader Section
BP	Base Pointer (Intel)
BP	push-button
BREQ	Bus Request
BSW	Barrel SWitch

C

C	Output Clock (*cf.* Clk)
C	Cycle
CAN	Controller Area Network
CC	Carry Clear
CCR	Condition Code Register
CCU	Computer Control Unit (*cf.* CU)
CD	Clock Domain
CDC	CD Crossing
CE	Chip Enable (*cf.* CS)
CERDIP	CERamic DIP
CF	Carry Flag
cGPU	computational GPU
CHMOS	Complementary High-density MOS (Intel)
CIR	Current Instruction Register
CISC	Complex Instruction Set Computer
CK	Input and Output Clock
Clk	Clock (*cf.* E)
CMOS	Complementary MOS (MOS complémentaire)
CMP	Chip MultiProcessing

CMT	Chip MultiThreading
COB	Chip On Board
COP	Computer Operating Properly (timer)
COSMAC	Complementary Symmetry Monolithic Array Computer
CP	CoProcessor
CP	Command Processor (AMD)
CP	Program Counter (*cf.* IP and PC)
CPGA	Ceramic PGA (Package)
CPSR	Current Program Status Register
CPU	Central Processing Unit
CR	Condition Register (*cf.* IR)
CR	Control Register
CRT	Cathode Ray Tube
CRU	Communication Register Unit
CS	Carry Set
CS	Chip Select (*cf.* CE)
CSR	Control and Status Register
CU	Control Unit
CWP	Current Window Pointer
CY	Carry Flag (8080A)

D

D	Data input
D	Decimal (flag)
D	Driver
D/A	Digital/Analog
DAC	Digital-to-Analog Converter
DAG	Data Address Generator, synonyms: ACU, AGU

DB	Differential Buffer
DC	Digit Carry flag (*cf.* AC, AF and H)
DC	Direct Current
DE	Denormalized operand Exception (x87)
DF	Direction Flag
DI	Destination Index (Intel)
DIL	Dual-In-Line
DIP	DIL Package
DLL	Delay-Locked Loop
DLX	DeLuXe
DMA	Data Memory Address (bus)
DMA	Direct Memory Access
DMD	Data Memory Data (bus)
DMI	Direct Media Interface (Intel)
DMUX	DeMUltipleXer
DQ	Data input/output
DR	Debug Register
DRAM	Dynamic RAM
DSO	Digital Storage Oscilloscope
DSP	Digital Signal Processor
DSP	Digital Signal Processing
DTACK	Data Transfer ACKnowledge (MC68000)

E

E	Clock signal (*cf.* Clk)
E	(Chip) Enable
EAE	Extended Arithmetic Element
EBI	External Bus Interface (MC68HC16)

ECL	Emitter Coupled Logic
EEPROM	Electrically EPROM
E2PROM	Electrically EPROM
ELGU	Equal, Less, Greater and Unordered
EPIC	Explicitly Parallel Instruction Computing
EPROM	Erasable PROM
EQ	EQual
ES	Error Summary (status) flag (x87)
EU	Execution Unit

F

F	Flag
FALU	Floating-Point ALU
FC	Function Code (MC68000)
FEEPROM	Flash EEPROM (definition JEDEC – JESD88C)
FET	Field Effect Transistor
FF	Flip-Flop
FFT	Fast Fourier Transform
FIR	Finite Impulse Response
FMA	Fused Multiply-Accumulate
FMAC	Fused MAC
FMUL	Floating-point MULtiplier
FPA	Floating-Point Accelerator core (IDT)
FPP	Floating-Point Processor
FPR	Floating-Point Register
FPU	Floating-Point Unit
FR4	Flame Retardant 4
FSB	Front-Side Bus

FSM	Finite-State Machine
FSR	Floating-point Status Register
FW	FirmWare
FXU	Fixed-Point Unit

G

GDT	Global Descriptor Table (Intel)
GDTR	GDT Register (Intel)
GE	(signed) Greater than or Equal
GPGPU	General-Purpose computing on GPU
GPL	General Purpose Logic
GPP	General-Purpose Processor
GPR	General-Purpose Register
GPU	Graphics Processing Unit
GT	Greater_Than

H

H	Half-carry (status) Flag (*cf.* AC, AF and DC)
H or h	High
HC	High-speed CMOS
HCMOS	High-speed CMOS
HD	Hard Disk
HDD	HD Drive
HDL	Hardware Description Language (*cf.* VHDL)
HI	Unsigned Higher
HIC	Heterogeneous InterConnect (IEEE)
HLL	High-Level (programming) Language
HMOS	High-density, High-performance or High-speed MOS (depletion-load NMOS)

| HMT | Hardware MultiThreading |
| HW | HardWare |

I

I	Input
I	Interrupt page address register or Interrupt vector (Z80)
IA	Intel Architecture
iAPX	Intel's Advanced Performance Architecture
IC	Interrupt Controller
IC	Integrated Circuit
ICC	Integer Condition Codes
ICU	Industrial Control Unit (Motorola MC14500B), i.e. PLC and UCI
ID	IDentification
ID	ID (flag)
IDT	Interrupt Descriptor Table (Intel)
IDTR	IDT Register (Intel)
IDU	Instruction Decoding Unit
IE	individual Interrupt Enable (PACE)
IE	Invalid operation Exception (x87)
IEN	Internet Engineering Note
IEN	master Interrupt Enable (PACE)
IEU	Instruction Execution Unit
IF	Interrupt enable Flag
IGP	Integrated Graphics Processor
IHS	Integrated Heat Spreader
I2C™	Inter Integrated Circuit
I2C™	Inter-IC
I2L	Integrated Injection Logic

IIO	Isolated I/O
IIR	Infinite Impulse Response
IIU	Instruction Issue Unit
I3L	Isoplanar I2L (Fairchild)
ILP	Instruction-Level Parallelism
ILR	Instruction-Location Register
IMP	Integrated MicroProcessor (NS)
IMUL	Integer MULtiplier
INT	INTerrupt (*cf.* IT)
I/O	Input/Output
IO	Input/Output (rarely used)
IOP	I/O Processor
IOPL	I/O Privilege Level (flag)
IoT	Internet of Things
IP	Instruction Pointer (Intel) (*cf.* CP and PC)
IP	Intellectual Property
IPU	Instruction Predecode Unit
IPU	Integer Processing Unit
IR	Index Register
IR	Indicator Register (*cf.* CR)
IR	Instruction Register
IRQ	Interrupt Request
IS	Instruction Set
IS	Interrupt Stack (*cf.* US)
ISA	Instruction Set Architecture
ISBN	International Standard Book Number
IT	InTerruption (i.e. INT)
IU	Integer Unit

J

| JTAG | Joint Test Action Group |

L

L or l	Low
LC	inductor L – capacitor C
LCC	(ceramic) Leadless Chip Carrier
LCD	Liquid Crystal Display
LDS	Lower Data Strobe
LDT	Local Descriptor Table (Intel)
LDTR	LDT Register (Intel)
LE	signed Less than or Equal/signed less or equal
LGA	Land Grid Array
LIFO	Last In, First Out
LIW	Long Instruction Word
LS	Unsigned Lower or Same
LSI	Large-Scale Integration
LSL	Logical Shift Left
LSR	Logical Shift Right
LT	Less_Than

M

M	Master
MAC	Multiply-and-ACcumulate
MAF	Multiply–Add–Fused (unit)
MAPS	Microprogrammable Arithmetic Processor System (NS)
MAR	Memory Address Register
MBR	Memory Buffer Register (*cf.* MDR)

MCS	Micro Computer Set (Intel)
MCU	Microprogram Control Unit
MCU	MicroController Unit (to prefer)
MCU	MicroComputer Unit
MDR	Memory Data Register (i.e. MBR)
MI	Minus
MIPS	Microprocessor without Interlocked Pipeline Stages of MIPS Technologies (then called MIPS Computer Systems)
MMIO	Memory-Mapped I/O
MMR	Memory-Mapped Register
MMU	Memory Management Unit
MMX	MultiMedia eXtensions (Intel)
MOS	Metal–Oxide Semiconductor
MPU	MicroProcessor Unit
MQ	Multiplier-Quotient Register
MS or M/S	Master/Slave(s)
MSb	Most Significant bit
MSI	Medium-Scale Integration
MSR	Model-Specific Register
MSW	Machine Status Word
MTRR	Memory Type Range Register
MUX	MUltipleXer

N

N	Negative (flag)
NB(C)	Natural Binary (Code)
NCU	Number Cruncher Unit
NE	Not Equal

NF	Negative Flag
NMI	Non-Maskable Interrupt
NMOS	Negative (channel) MOS
NT	Nested Task (flag)

O

O	Output
OCR	Output Compare Register
OE	numerical Overflow Exception (x87)
OF	Overflow Flag (*cf.* VF)
OoO	Out-of-Order
OS	Operating System
OTP	One-Time Programmable
OTPROM	One-Time EPROM

P

PACE	Processing and Control Element (NS)
PC	Performance Computing
PC	Personal Computer
PC	Program Counter (*cf.* CP and IP)
PCB	Printed Circuit Board
PCI	Peripheral Component Interconnect (standard)
PCU	Program Control Unit (*cf.* DSP from Motorola)
PDP	Programmable Data Processor (DEC)
PE	inexact-result or Precision Exception (x87)
PF	Parity Flag
PGA	Pin Grid Array (Package)
PIC	Peripheral Interface Controller (General Instrument)

PIC	Programmable Intelligent Computer (General Instrument)
PIC	Programmable Interrupt Controller
PL	PLus
PLA	Programmable Logic Array
PLC	Programmable Logic Controller (Motorola MC14500B), *cf.* ICU
PLCC	Plastic (J-)Leaded Chip Carrier (JEDEC)
PLD	Programmable Logic Device
PLL	Phase-Locked Loop
PMA	Program Memory Address
PMD	Program Memory Data
PMM	Power Management Modes
PMOS	Positive (channel) MOS
POR	Power-On Reset
POWER	Performance Optimization with Enhanced RISC
PowerPC	POWER Performance Computing
PPS	Programmed Processor System
PRISM	Parallel Reduced Instruction Set Machine (DEC Alpha AXP)
PROM	Programmable ROM
PSR	Processor Status Register
PSW	Program Status Word
PTR	PoinTer Register
PU	Processing Unit
PWM	Pulse Width Modulation

Q

Q	Data output or data to write (Data Output)
Q	Quartz

Q	Overflow flag (ARMv5)
QFP	Quad Flat Package or FlatPak package (NS)
QIL	Quad-In-Line
QIP	QIL Package

R

R	Read
R	Memory Refresh Register (Z80)
R	Result (bus)
RAM	Random Access Memory
RBP	Register Bank Protect
RC	Resistor–Capacitor
RCU	Refresh Control Unit
RF	Resume Flag
RF	Register File
RISC	Reduced Instruction Set Computer
RMW	Read–Modify–Write
ROB	ReOrder Buffer
ROL	ROtate Left
ROM	Read-Only Memory
ROR	ROtate Right
RS	Recommended Standard
RS	RISC System
RSC-Forth	Rockwell Single-Chip Forth
RST	ReSeT
RT	Register Transfer (i.e. RTL)
RTC	Real-Time Clock

RTL	RT Language (to prefer rather than RT Level)
R/#W or R/WE	Read/Write

S

S	hardware Stack pointer (MC6809)
S	Schottky
S	Set
S	Signal
S	Slave
S	Exit
SATA	Serial ATA
SAW	Surface Acoustic Wave
SCC	Single-Chip microcomputer
SCCC	Single-Chip Cloud Computer (Intel)
SC/MP	Simple Cost-effective Chip MicroProcessor (NS)
SDRAM	Synchronous DRAM
SF	Sign Flag
SF	Stack Fault (x87)
SFR	Special Function Register
SFU	Special Function Unit
SI	Source Index (Intel)
SIPO	Serial-In Parallel-Out
SISC	Special Instruction Set Computer
SMB	System Management Bus
SMT	Simultaneous MultiThreading
SO	Summary Overflow
SoC	System on (a) Chip, System-on-Chip
SP	Stack Pointer

SPARC	Scalable Processor ARChitecture
SPI™	Serial Peripheral Interface
SPM	ScratchPad Memory
SPR	Special (Purpose) Register
SR	Shift Register
SR	Status (flag) Register
SRAM	Static RAM
SSD	Solid-State Disk
SSHD	Solid-State Hybrid Drive
SSRAM	Synchronous SRAM
ST	Status Register (TMS 9900)
SVS	Supply-Voltage Supervisor
SW	SoftWare
SWP	Saved Window Pointer

T

TDP	Thermal Design Power
TF	Trap Flag
TLB	Translation Lookaside Buffer
TLP	Thread-Level Parallelism
TOP	Top-of-Stack Pointer (x87)
TPU	Time Processor Unit
TR	Task Register
TR	Test Register
TRAM	TRAnsputer Module
TTL	Transistor–Transistor Logic

U

U	User stack pointer (MC6809)
UDS	Upper Data Strobe
UE	numerical Underflow Exception (x87)
UMIP	User-Mode Instruction Prevention
UPSR	User PSR
US	User Stack (*cf.* IS)
USB	Universal Serial Bus

V

VAN	Vehicle Area Network
VAX	Virtual Addressed eXtended (DEC)
VC	no oVerflow
VCXO	Voltage-Controlled Crystal Oscillator
VDC	Video Display Coprocessor
VF	oVerflow Flag (*cf.* OF)
VHDL	VHSIC HDL
VHSIC	Very High Speed Integrated Circuit
VIF	Virtual Interrupt Flag
VIP	Virtual Interrupt Pending (flag)
VLIW	Very LIW
VLSI	Very LSI
VM	Virtual Memory
VM	Virtual-8086 Mode (flag)
VS	oVerflow

W

W	Wait
W	Write
WDI	WatchDog Input
WDO	WatchDog Output
WDT	WatchDog Timer
WE	Write Enable
WIM	Window Invalid Mask (SPARC)
WP	Workspace Pointer (TMS 9900)
WS	Wait State

X

X	eXtend bit (MC68000)
XCC	eXtended Condition Codes
XER	fiXed-point Exception Register (PowerPC)

Z

Z	High-impedance state (Hi-Z)
ZCD	Zero-Crossing Detector
ZE	Zero divide Exception (x87)
ZF	Zero Flag

Other

μC	microcontroller
μP	microprocessor
2D or 2-D	two-dimensional
3D or 3-D	three-dimensional

Units of measurement or unit prefixes

b/s or bps	bit(s) per second
G	giga (= 10^9)
Gib	gibibit
Gibi	gigabinary (prefix Gi = 2^{30})
GiB	gibibyte
GHZ	gigahertz
IPC	Instructions Per Cycle
k	kilo (= 1000)
K	binary kilo (= 1024) – old prefix to avoid, the capital letter made it possible to distinguish the value of the prefix. Choice not retained in this work
Kb	kilobit (= 1024 b) – old multiple to avoid
KB	kilobyte (1024 bytes) – old multiple to avoid
kHz	kilohertz
Kib	kibibit
Kibi	kilobinary (prefix Ki = 2^{10})
KiB	kibibyte
M	mega (= 10^6)
Mb	megabit
Mb/s or Mbps	megabit per second
Mebi	megabinary (prefix Mi = 2^{20})
MHz	megahertz
Mib	mebibit
MiB	mebibyte
MIPS	Million Instructions Per second
Tebi	tebibinary (prefix Ti = 2^{40})
Tib	tebibit
TiB	tebibyte

Voltage characteristics

Gnd	Ground
V_{CC}	Collector DC supply voltage
V_{DC}	DC voltage
V_{DD}	Drain DC supply voltage
V_{SS}	Source–Source voltage

Current characteristics

I_{CC}	supply current
I_{DD}	supply current

Power characteristics

P_D	Dynamic power
P_L	capacitive-Load Power
P_S	Static power
P_T	Transient power
P_{tot}	total power

Temporal characteristics

t_a	access time
t_{acc} or t_{ACC}	access time
t_{AD}	Address Delay time
t_{AH}	Address Hold time
t_{AV}	Address Valid time to E (rise)
t_c or t_{cyc}	cycle time
t_{DDW}	Write Data Delay time
t_{DHR}	Read Data Hold time
t_{DHW}	Write Data Hold time

t_{DSR}	Read Data Setup time
t_f	fall time
t_h or t_{hold}	hold time
t_{pd}	propagation delay time
t_{PLHM}	Propagation delay time, Low-to-High level
t_{PWM}	Pulse Width
t_r	rise time
t_{su} or t_{setup}	setup time
t_{THLM}	Transition time, High-to-Low level
t_{TLHM}	Transition time, Low-to-High level
t_w	pulse duration (width)
t_w	write time
t_{wc}	write cycle time
t_{wr}	write release time

Company or organization

ACM	Association for Computing Machinery
AFIPS	American Federation of Information Processing Societies
AFISI	*Association Française d'Ingénierie des Systèmes d'Information* (French Association for Information Systems Engineering)
AMD	Advanced Micro Devices, Inc.
AMI	American Microsystems, Inc.
ANSI	American National Standards Institute
ARM	Acorn RISC Machine then Advanced RISC Machines
CEI	*Commission Electrotechnique* Internationale (International Electrotechnical Commission) (i.e. IEC)
DEC	Digital Equipment Corporation
EFCIS	Study and Manufacture of Special Integrated Circuits

HP	Hewlett-Packard
IBM	International Business Machines Corporation
IEC	International Electrotechnical Commission (i.e. CEI)
IEEE	Institute of Electrical and Electronics Engineers
ISO	International Organization for Standardization, Organisation Internationale de Standardisation
ISSCC	IEEE International Solid-State Circuits Conference
JEDEC	Joint Electron Device Engineering Council (Solid-State Technology Association)
MIL	Microsystems International Limited
MITS	Micro Instrumentation Telemetry Systems
MPR	Microprocessor Report
NS	National Semiconductor
RCA	Radio Corporation of America
TI	Texas Instruments
WDC	Western Digital Corporation, Western Digital Center

™ – trademark

I^2C	Philips
i486	Intel Corporation
MCS	Intel
Pentium	Intel Corporation
SPI	Motorola
VAX	Digital Equipment Corporation

® – registered trademark

AMD	AMD
Arm	Arm Limited
Atmel	Microchip

AVR	Microchip
DEC	Digital Equipment Corporation
Fairchild	Fairchild Semiconductor Corporation
Intel	Intel
PDP	Digital Equipment Corporation
Pentium	Intel
PIC	Microchip Technology
TRI-STATE	NS
Xeon	Intel

References

Preface

Darche, P. (2000). *Architecture des ordinateurs – Représentation des nombres et codes – Cours avec exercices corrigés*. Éditions Gaëtan Morin, November.

Darche, P. (2002). *Architecture des ordinateurs – Fonctions booléennes, logiques combinatoire et séquentielle – Cours avec exercices et exemples en VHDL*. Éditions Vuibert, March.

Darche, P. (2003). *Architecture des ordinateurs – Interfaces et périphériques – Cours avec exercices corrigés*. Éditions Vuibert, June.

Darche, P. (2004). *Architecture des ordinateurs – Logique booléenne: implémentations et technologies*. Éditions Vuibert, November.

Darche, P. (2012). *Mémoires à semi-conducteurs: Principe de fonctionnement et organisation interne des mémoires vives – Volume 1*. Éditions Vuibert. January. Un des quatre ouvrages sélectionnés pour le prix AFISI (Association Française d'Ingénierie des Systèmes d'Information) du meilleur livre informatique.

Chapter 1 to 6

Agrawal, A. and Garner, R.B. (1992). SPARC: A scalable processor architecture. *Future Generation Computer Systems*, 7(2–3), 303–309. April.

Alsup, M. (1990). Motorola's 88000 family architecture. *IEEE Micro*, 10(3), 48–66.

Altman, L. (1974). Single-chip microprocessors open up a new world of applications. Technical articles. *Electronics*, 47(8), 81–87. April 18.

AMD (1987). Am 29000 Streamlined Instruction Processor User's Manual. Advanced Micro Devices.

Analog Devices (1990). In *Digital Signal Processing Using the ADSP-2100 Family*, Mar, A. (ed.). The Applications Engineering Staff of Analog Devices, DSP Division. Prentice Hall.

Anlauff, H., Böttcher, A., and Ruckert, M. (2002). *Das MMIX-Buch: Ein praxisnaher Zugang zur Informatik*. Springer-Verlag.

Bartee, T.C. and Chapman, D.J. (1965). Design of an accumulator for a general purpose computer. *IEEE Transactions on Electronic Computers*, EC 14(4), 570–574. August.

Bassett, R.K. (2002). *To the Digital Age: Research Labs, Start-up Companies, and the Rise of MOS Technology*. Johns Hopkins Studies in the History of Technology. Johns Hopkins University Press.

Bayliss, J.A., Colley, S.R., Kravitz, R.H., McCormick, G.A., Richardson, W.S., Wilde, D.K., and Wittmer, L.L. (1981). The instruction decoding unit for the VLSI 432 general data processor. *IEEE Journal of Solid-State Circuits (JSSC)*, SC-16(5), 531–537. October.

Becker, M.C., Allen, M.S., Moore, C.R., Muhich, J.S., and Tuttle, D.P. (1993). The powerPC 601 microprocessor. *IEEE Micro*, 13(5), 54–68. October.

Bell, C.G. (2008a). Bell's law for the birth and death of computer classes. *Communications of the ACM (CACM)*, 51(1) 50th Anniversary Issue: 1958–2008, 86–94. January.

Bell, C.G. (2008b). Bell's Law for the birth and death of computer classes: A theory of the computer's evolution. *IEEE Solid-State Circuits Society Newsletter (SSCS)*, 13(4), 8–19. Fall.

van Berkel C.H. (Kees), Josephs, M.B., and Nowick, S.M. (1999). Scanning the technology. *Proceedings of IEEE*, 87(2) Special Issue on Asynchronous Circuits and Systems, 223–233. February.

Birnbaum, J.S. and Worley, W.S. Jr. (1985). Beyond RISC: High-precision architecture. *Hewlett-Packard Journal (HPJ)*, 36(8), 4–10. August.

Birnbaum, J.S. and Worley, W.S. Jr. (1986). Beyond RISC: High-precision architecture. *31st IEEE Computer Society International Conference (Spring COMPCON'86)*, 40–47. March 3–6. San Francisco, California, USA. Also in Stallings 1986, 253–260.

Boland, K. and Dollas, A. (1994). Predicting and precluding problems with memory latency. *IEEE Micro*, 14(4), 59–67. August.

Booher, R.K. (1968). MOS GP computer. *1968 Fall Joint Computer Conference (AFIPS'68)*, Part I, 877–889. December 9–11. San Francisco, California, USA.

Boone, G. (1973). Computing systems CPU. American patent no. 3757306. Application number: 05/176668. Filing date: August 31. Publication date: September 4, 1973.

Boone, G.W. and Cochran, MJ. (1978). Variable function programmed calculator. American patent no. 4074351. Application number: 05/771498. Filing date: February 24, 1977. Publication date: February 14.

Buchanan, J.K. (1976). MOS DC voltage booster circuit. Application number: 05/475366. Filing date: June 3, 1974. Publication date: March 2.

Burroughs (1956). Handbook Central Computer. DATATRON Electronic Data Processing Systems. Burroughs Corporation. March.

Carter, J.W. (1995). *Microprocessor Architecture and Microprogramming: A State-Machine Approach*. Prentice Hall International Limited, London.

Catanzaro, B.J. (1991). In *The SPARC Technical Papers*, Catanzaro, B.J. (ed.). Sun Technical Reference Library. Sun Microsystems, Inc. Springer-Verlag New York.

Cherupalli, H., Duwe, H., Ye, W., Kumar R., and Sartori J. (2017). Bespoke processors for applications with ultra-low area and power constraints. *44th Annual International Symposium on Computer Architecture (ISCA'17)*, 41–54. June 24–28, 2017. Toronto, Ontario, Canada. *ACM SIGARCH Computer Architecture News*, 45(2) – ISCA'17, 41–54. May.

Clark, W.A. (1967). Macromodular computer systems. *1967 Spring Joint Computer Conference (AFIPS'67)*, 335–336. April 18–20, 1967. Atlantic City, New Jersey, USA.

Cohen, D. (1981). On holy wars and a plea for peace. *IEEE Computer*, 14(10), 48–54. October 1981. Original: IEN (Internet Engineering Note) 137. USC/ISI (University of Southern California /Information Sciences Institute). April 1.

Computers and Automation (1968). Viatron System 21 advertising. *Computers and Automation*, 17(12), 42. December.

Cragon, H.G. (1980). The elements of single-chip microcomputer architecture. *IEEE Computer*, 13(10), 27–41. October.

Crawford, J. (1986). Architecture of the Intel 80386. *1986 International Conference on Computer Design (ICCD'86)*, 155–160. October 1986. Republished in Hill *et al.* 2000, 156–162.

Cruz, J.L., González, A., Valero, M., and Topham, N.P. (2000). Multiple-banked register file architectures. *27th Annual International Symposium on Computer Architecture (ISCA '00)*, 316–325. June 10–14 2000. Vancouver, British Columbia, Canada. *ACM SIGARCH Computer Architecture News*, 28(2) Special Issue, 316–325. May.

Cushman, R.H. (1975). 2-1/2-generation µP's-$10 parts that perform like low-end mini's. EDN µP Design Series. *EDN*, 36–41. September 20.

Dannenberg, R.B. (1979). An architecture with many operand registers to efficiently execute block-structured languages. *6th Annual Symposium on Computer Architecture (ISCA'79)*, 50–57. April 23–25.

Darche, P. (2000). *Architecture des ordinateurs – Représentation des nombres et codes – Cours avec exercices corrigés*. Éditions Gaëtan Morin. November.

Darche, P. (2002). *Architecture des ordinateurs – Fonctions booléennes, logiques combinatoire et séquentielle – Cours avec exercices et exemples en VHDL.* Éditions Vuibert. March.

Darche, P. (2003). *Architecture des ordinateurs – Interfaces et périphériques – Cours avec exercices corrigés.* Éditions Vuibert. June.

Darche, P. (2004). *Architecture des ordinateurs – Logique booléenne: Implémentations et technologies.* Éditions Vuibert. November.

Darche, P. (2012). *Mémoires à semi-conducteurs: Principe de fonctionnement et organisation interne des mémoires vives – Volume 1.* Éditions Vuibert. January. Un des quatre ouvrages sélectionnés pour le prix AFISI (Association Française d'Ingénierie des Systèmes d'Information) du meilleur livre informatique.

Davis, R.L. (1969). The ILLIAC IV processing element. *IEEE Transactions on Computers,* C-18(9), 800–816. September.

Davis, R.L. (1974). Uniform shift networks. *IEEE Computer,* 7(9), 60–71. September.

Diefendorf, K. and Silha, E. (1994). The powerPC user instruction set architecture. *IEEE Micro,* 14(5), 30–41. October.

El-Ayat, K.A. (1979). Special feature. The Intel 8089: An integrated I/O processor. *IEEE Computer,* 12(6), 67–78. June.

El-Ayat, K.A. and Agarwal, R.K. (1985). The Intel 80386 – architecture and implementation. *IEEE Micro,* 5(6), 4–22. December.

Elliott, W.S., Owen, C.E., Devonald, C.H., and Maudsley, B.G. (1956). The design philosophy of pegasus, a quantity-production computer. *Proceedings of the IEE – Part B: Radio and Electronic Engineering,* 103(2), Part S, 188–196. October.

Fairchild (1976). Macrologic Bipolar Microprocessor Databook. Fairchild.

Floating Point Systems (1979). *AP-120B Processor Handbook.* Floating Point Systems, Inc. February. Republished in Kuhn and Padua 1981.

Forsell, M.J. (1996). Minimal pipeline architecture – an alternative to superscalar architecture. *Microprocessors and Microsystems,* 20(5), 277–284. September.

Forward Concepts (2008). Wireless/DSP market bulletin. Forward concepts. February 4.

Fox, W.A. and Reyling, G.F. Jr. (1975). A single chip 16-bit microprocessor for general application. *Microelectronics Reliability,* 14(4) Special Seminex'75 edition, 389–397.

Franklin, M.A. and Pan, T. (1993). Clocked and asynchronous instruction pipelines. *26th Annual International Symposium on Microarchitecture (MICRO 26),* 177–184. December 1–3. Austin, Texas, USA.

Frantz, G.A, Lin, K.-S., Reimer, J.B., and Bradley, J. (1986). The Texas instruments TMS320C25 digital signal microcomputer. *IEEE Micro,* 6(6), 10–28. December.

Fu, B., Saini, A., and Gelsinger, P. (1990). Performance and microarchitecture of the i486™ processor. *1989 IEEE International Conference on Computer Design: VLSI in Computers and Processors (ICCD'89)*, 182–187. October 2–4. Cambridge, MA, USA.

Garner, R.B., Agrawal, A., Briggs, F., Brown, E.W., Hough, D., Joy, B., Kleiman, S., Muchnick, S., Namjoo, M., Patterson, D., Pendleton, J., and Tuck, R. (1988). The scalable processor architecture (SPARC). *33rd IEEE Computer Society International Computer Conference (Compcon Spring'88)*, 278–283. 29 February 29 – March 3 1988.

Gay, C. (1984). The MC68020, a true 32-bit microprocessor. *Microprocessors and Microsystems*, 8(7), 377–383. September.

Goossens, B. (2003). The instruction register file. *2003 International Conference on Parallel Computing Technologies (PaCT 2003)*. Lecture Notes in Computer Science (LNCS), 2763, 467–481.

Goossens, B. and Defour, D. (2005). The instruction register file micro-architecture. *Future Generation Computer Systems*, 21(5), 767–773. May.

Gregory, V.C. (1979). Industrial control processor. American patent no. 4153942. Assignee: Motorola, Inc. Application number: 761738. Filing date: January 24. Publication date: May 8.

Jim Gray and Preshant Shenay (1999). "Rules of Thumb in Data Engineering". Technical Report MS-TR-99-100. Microsoft Research Advanced Technology Division. Microsoft Corporation. December 1999. *16th International Conference on Data Engineering (ICDE '00)*, 3-10. February 28 - March 03, 2000.

Grohoski, G.F. (1990). Machine organization of the IBM RISC system/6000 processor. *IBM Journal of Research and Development*, 34(1), 37–58. January.

Halfhill, T.R. (2006). The intel 4004's 35th anniversary. *Microprocessor Report (MPR)*, no. 121806. December 18.

Halfill, T.R. (2009). How Intel got big. *Microprocessor Report (MPR)*, 8, February 17.

Hall, M. and Barry, J. (1990). In *The Sun Technology Papers*, Hall, M. and Barry, J. (eds). Sun Technical Reference Library. Sun Microsystems, Inc. Springer Verlag New York.

Heering, J. (1980). The Intel 8086, the Zilog Z8000, and the motorola MC68000 microprocessors. *Euromicro Newsletter*, 6(3), 135–143. May.

Helbig, W.A. and Stringer, J.D. (1977). A VLSI microcomputer: The RCA ATMAC. *IEEE Computer*, 10(9), 22–29. September.

Hennessy, J.L. (1984). VLSI processor architecture. *IEEE Transactions on Computers*, C-33(12), 1221–1246. December.

Hennessy, J.L. and Patterson, D.A. (2011). *Computer Architecture. A Quantitative Approach*, 15th edition. The Morgan Kaufmann Series in Computer Architecture and Design. September.

Hennessy, J., Jouppi, N., Baskett, F., Gross, T., and Gill, J. (1982a). Hardware/Software tradeoffs for increased performance. *First International Symposium on Architectural Support for Programming Languages and Operating Systems (ASPLOS I)*, 2–11. *ACM SIGARCH Computer Architecture News*, 10(2), 2–11. March. *ACM SIGPLAN Notices*, 17(4), 2–11. April.

Hennessy, J., Jouppi, N., Przybylski, S.A., Rowen, C., Gross, T., Baskett, F., and Gill, J. (1982b). MIPS: A microprocessor architecture. *15th Annual Workshop on Microprogramming on Microprogramming*, 17–22. October 1982. Palo Alto, California, United States.

Hennig, F., Hingarh, H.K., O'Brien, D., and Verhofstadt, P.W.J. (1977). Isoplanar integrated injection logic: A high-performance bipolar technology. *IEEE Journal of Solid-State Circuits (JSSC)*, 12(2), 101–109. April.

Hill, M.D., Jouppi, N.P., and Sohi, G.S. (2000). In *Readings in Computer Architecture*, Hill, M.D., Jouppi, N.P., and Sohi, G.S. (eds). Morgan Kaufmann Publishers Inc.

Hirki, M., Ou, Z., Khan, K.N., Nurminen, J.K., and Niemi, T. (2016). Empirical study of the power consumption of the x86-64 instruction decoder. *2016 USENIX Workshop on Cool Topics in Sustainable Data Centers (CoolDC'16)*. Santa Clara, CA, USA, March 19.

Hitchcock, S.M. (1990). SPARC: Architecture to implementations. *Microprocessors and Microsystems*, 14(6), 417–420. July/August.

Hokenek, E., Montoye, R.K., and Cook, P.W. (1990). Second-generation RISC floating point with multiply-add fused. *IEEE Journal of Solid-State Circuits (JSSC)*, 25(5), 1207–1213. October.

Huguet, M. and Lang, T. (1985). A reduced register file for RISC architectures. *ACM SIGARCH Computer Architecture News*, 13(4), 22–31.

Huntzicker, S., Dayringer, M., Soprano, J., Weerasinghe, A, Harris, D.M., and Patil, D. (2008). Energy-delay tradeoffs in 32-bit static shifter designs. *IEEE International Conference on Computer Design (ICCD 2008)*, 626–632. October 12–15.

Hyatt, G.P. (1990). Single chip integrated circuit computer architecture. American patent no. US4942516. Application number: 07/209115. Filing date: June 17, 1988. Publication date: July 17.

IEEE (1985). IEEE Standard for Binary Floating-Point Arithmetic. ANSI/IEEE Std 754-1985. Republished in SIGPLAN Notices, 22(2), 9–25. February.

IEEE (1995). IEEE Standard for Heterogeneous Interconnect (HIC) (Low-Cost, Low-Latency Scalable Serial Interconnect for Parallel System Construction). IEEE Std 1355-1995, 21 September.

IEEE (1996). The microprocessor is 25. *IEEE Micro*, 16(2). April.

IEEE (2000). IEEE Standard for Heterogeneous Interconnect (HIC) (Low-Cost, Low-Latency Scalable Serial Interconnect for Parallel System Construction). IEEE Std 1355-1995 (withdrawn 2005). ISO/IEC Std 14575:2000.

IEEE (2002). IEEE Standard for a Control and Status Registers (CSR) Architecture for Microcomputer Buses. IEEE Std 1212™-2001 (Revision of IEEE Std 1212-1994). Approved 6 December 2001, September 6.

IEEE (2008). IEEE Standard for Floating-Point Arithmetic. IEEE Std 754™-2008. Revision of IEEE Std 754-1985. August 29.

IEEE (2015). Energy Efficient Digital – 2015 Trends. ISSCC (International Solid-State Circuits Conference) Press Kit. San Francisco, CA, USA. February 22–26.

Intel (1972). 8008 8-bit parallel central processing unit – users manual. *MCS-8 Micro Computer Set. Rev. 2.* Intel Corporation. November.

Intel (1973). MCS-4 Micro Computer Set User Manual. Intel Corporation. February.

Intel (1976). Data Catalog 1976. Intel Corporation.

Intel (1977, 1978). MCS-48™ Microcomputer User's Manual. Intel Corporation. July.

Intel (1981). Systems Data Catalog. Intel Corporation. January.

Intel (1983). The MCS®-80/85 Family User's Manual. Order Number: 205775-002. Intel Corporation. January.

Intel (1989). 8086/8088 User's Manual, Programmer's and Hardware Reference. Intel.

Intel (1992). Intel486™ DX Microprocessor Data Book. Intel Corporation.

Intel (2003). IA-32 Intel® Architectures Software Developer's Manual, Volume 1: Basic Architecture. Intel Corporation.

Intel (2006). Intel® 64 and IA-32 Architectures Software Developer's Manual, Volume 1: Basic Architecture. Intel Corporation. November.

Intel (2013). Desktop 3rd Generation Intel® Core™ Processor Family, Desktop Intel® Pentium® Processor Family, and Desktop Intel® Celeron® Processor Family. Datasheet – Volume 1 of 2. Document Number: 326764-008. November.

Intel (2018). 7th Generation Intel® Processor Families for S Platforms and Intel® Core™ X-Series Processor Family. Datasheet, Volume 1 of 2. Revision 003. Document Number: 335195-003. Intel Corporation. December.

Jouppi, N.P. (1989). The nonuniform distribution of instruction-level and machine parallelism and its effect on performance. *IEEE Transactions on Computers*, 38(12), 1645–1658. December.

Kane, G. (1988). *MIPS RISC Architecture*. Prentice-Hall, Inc.

Katevenis, M.G.H, Sherburne, R., Patterson, D.A., and Séquin, C.A. (1983). The RISC II micro-architecture. *IFIP TC10/WG10.5 International Conference on Very Large Scale Integration (VLSI '83)*, 349–359. Trondheim, Norway. Also published in *the Journal of VLSI and Computer Systems*, 1(2), 1984. Computer Science Press Inc. 16–19 August.

Kim, H.H., Hwang, S.H., and Kyung, C.M. (1993). A practical design method for instruction decoder PLAs for microprogrammed controllers. *Microprocessors and Microsystems*, 17(8), 481–488. October.

Kloker, K.L. (1986). The Motorola DSP56000 digital signal processor. *IEEE Micro*, 6(6), 29–48. December.

Knuth, D.E. (1968). *The Art of Computer Programming. Volume 1 / Fundamental Algorithms*. Addison-Wesley Series in Computer Science and Information Processing, Addison-Wesley Publishing Company.

Knuth, D.E. (1999). In *MMIXware – A RISC Computer for the Third Millennium*. Goos, G., Hartmanis, J., and van Leeuwen, J. (eds). Lecture Notes in Computer Science (LNCS), 1750.

Knuth, D.E. (2004). *The Art of Computer Programming – Fascicle 1*. Addison-Wesley.

Kuhn, R.H. and Padua, D.A. (1981). In *Tutorial on Parallel Processing*, Kuhn, R.H. and Padua, D.A. (eds). IEEE Press.

Kunt, M. (1981). *Traitement numérique des signaux*. Traité d'électricité, vol. XX. Ecole Polytechnique Fédérale de Lausanne. Presses Polytechniques Romandes.

Lampson, B.W. (1982). Fast procedure calls. First International Symposium on Architectural Support for Programming Languages and Operating Systems (ASPLOS I), 66–76. Palo Alto, California (CA), United States. ACM SIGARCH Computer Architecture News, 10(2), 66–76. March 1-3 1982. ACM SIGPLAN Notices, 17(4). *Proceedings of the 1982 Symposium on Architectural Support for Programming Languages and Operating Systems*, 66–76. April 1982.

Lavington, S.H. (1980). *Early British Computers*. Manchester University Press.

Lin, K-S., Frantz, G.A., and Simar, R. (1987). The TMS320 family of digital signal processors. *Proceedings of the IEEE*, 75(9), 1143–1159. September.

Liu, J., Bell, B., and Truong, T. (2006). Analysis and characterization of Intel Itanium instruction bundles for improving VLIW processor performance. *First International Multi-Symposiums on Computer and Computational Sciences (IMSCCS'06)*. Hanzhou, Zhejiang, China. June 20–24.

Lucas, M.S.P and Sobering, T.J. (1983). Low-power operation of the SBP9989 16-Bit I^2L processor. *IEEE Transactions on Instrumentation and Measurement*, 32(4), 509–512. December.

MacGregor, D., Mothersole, D., and Moyer, B. (1984). The motorola MC68020. *IEEE Micro*, 4(4), 101–118. July/August.

Madisetti, V.K. (1995). *VLSI Digital Signal Processors: An Introduction to Rapid Prototyping and Design Synthesis*. Butterworth-Heinemann and IEEE Press.

Magar, S.S., Caudel, E.R., and Leigh, A.W. (1982). A microcomputer with digital signal processing capability. *1982 IEEE International Solid-State Circuits Conference (ISSCC'82)*, XXV, 32–33. San Francisco, CA, USA. February 10–12.

Martin, A.J., Burns, S.M., Lee, T.K., Borkovic, D., and Hazewindus, P.J. (1989). The design of an asynchronous microprocessor. *ACM SIGARCH Computer Architecture News*, 17(4), 99–110. June.

Mazor, S. (1995). The history of the microcomputer – invention and evolution. *Proceedings of the IEEE*, 83(12), 1601–1608. December.

McKenzie, K. (1976). A structured approach to microcomputer system design. Behavior *Research Methods & Instrumentation*, 8(2), 123–128.

McLellan, E. (1993). The alpha AXP architecture and 21064 processor. *IEEE Micro*, 13(3), 36–47. May/June.

Microcomputer Digest (1975). 3rd Generation microprocessor. *Microcomputer Digest*, 2(2), 1–3. Microcomputer Associates. August.

MIPS (2005). MIPS64® Architecture for programmers. Volume I: Introduction to the MIPS64® architecture. Document Number: MD00083, Revision 2.50. MIPS Technologies, Inc. July 1.

Montoye, R.K., Hokenek, E., and Runyon, S.L. (1990). Design of the IBM RISC system/6000 floating-point execution unit. *IBM Journal of Research and Development*, 34(1), 59–70. January.

Moore, C.R. (1993). The powerPC 601 microprocessor. *1993 IEEE International Computer Conference (COMPCON Spring'93)*, 109–116. San Francisco, CA, USA. February 22–26.

Moore, G.E. (2003). No exponential is forever: but "Forever" can be delayed!. *2003 IEEE International Solid-State Circuits Conference (ISSCC 2003)*, 20–23. 10. San Francisco, USA. February 9–13.

Moore, S.K. (2017). Bespoke processors: A new path to cheap Chips (News). *IEEE Spectrum*, 54(8), 11–12. August.

Mori, R., Tajima, H., Tajima, M., and Okada, Y. (1977). Microprocessors in Japan. *Euromicro Newsletter*, 3(4), 50–57. October.

Motorola (1992). MC68020/MC68EC020 Microprocessors User's Manual. Motorola Inc.

Motorola (1993). PowerPC™ 601 RISC Microprocessor User's Manual. Reference: MPC601UM/AD. Motorola Inc.

Moussouris, J.P., Crudele, L.M., Freitas, D., Hansen, C., Hudson, E., Mars, R., Przybylski, S.A., Riordan, T., Rowen, C., and Hof, D.V. (1986). A CMOS RISC processor with integrated system functions. *31st IEEE Computer Society International Conference (Spring COMPCON'86)*, 126–131. San Francisco, California, USA. March 3–6.

Namjoo. M. (1989). SPARC implementations: ASIC vs. custom design. *22nd Annual Hawaii International Conference on System Sciences*, vol. I: Architecture Track, 19–22. 3–6 January.

Nicoud, J.-D. (1991). *Microprocessor Interface Design – Digital Circuits and Concepts.* Chapman & Hall and Masson.

Noyce, R.N. and Hoff, M.E. Jr. (1981). A history of microprocessor development at Intel. *IEEE Micro*, 1(1), 8–21. February.

NS (1976). SC/MP technical description. Publication Number 4200079A. National Semiconductor Corporation. January.

NS (1978). INS8060 Single-Chip 8-bit N-Channel Microprocessor (SC/MP Family). National Semiconductor. January.

O'Connell, F.P. and White, S.W. (2000). POWER3: The next generation of PowerPC processors. *IBM Journal of Research and Development*, 44(6), 873–884. November.

Oehler, R.R. and Groves, R.D. (1990). IBM RISC system/6000 processor architecture. *IBM Journal of Research and Development*, 34(1), 23–36. January.

Oehmke, D.W., Binkert, N.L., Mudge, T., and Reinhardt, S.K. (2005). How to fake 1000 registers. *38th Annual IEEE/ACM International Symposium on Microarchitecture (MICRO-38)*, 7–18. November.

Ogdin, J. (1975). Microprocessor scorecard. *Euromicro Newsletter*, 1(2), 43–77. January.

Palmer, J., Nave, R., Wymore, C., Koehler, R., and McMinn, C. (1980). Making mainframe mathematics accessible to microcomputers. *Electronics*, 53, 114–121. May 8, 1980. Republished in *Electronics Book Series. Microprocessors and Microcomputers – One-chip Controllers to High-end Systems*, 254–261.

Patterson, D.A (1984). RISC watch. *ACM SIGARCH Computer Architecture News*, 12(1), 11–19. Also in Stallings 1986, p. 321–329. March.

Peddle, C.I., Mathys, W.L., Mensch, W.D. Jr., and Orgill, R.H. (1976). Integrated circuit microprocessor with parallel binary adder having on-the-fly correction to provide decimal results. American patent no. 3991307. Application number: 05/613890. Filing date: November 9, 1975. Publication date: September 16.

Petritz, R.L. (1977). The pervasive microprocessor: Trends and prospects. *IEEE Spectrum*, 14(7), 18–24. July.

Powers, I. (1978). MC6809 microprocessor. Microprocessors, 2(3), 162. July.

Quach, L. and Chueh, R. (1988). CMOS gate array implementation of SPARC. *23 IEEE Computer Society International Conference (COMPCON Spring'88)*, 15–17. San Francisco, CA, USA. 29 February 29 – March 3.

Quatse, J.T. and Keir, R.A. (1967). A parallel accumulator for a general-purpose computer. *IEEE Transactions on Electronic Computers*, EC 16(2), 165–171. April.

Rallapalli, K. and Verhofstadt, P. (1975). MACROLOGIC: Versatile functional blocks for high performance digital systems. *1975 National Computer Conference and Exposition (AFIPS '75)*, 67–73. Anaheim, California, USA. May 19–22.

RCA (1975). User Manual for the COSMAC Microprocessor. RCA Solid State Division.

Richardson, W.S., Bayliss, J.A., Colley, S.R., Kravitz, R.H., McCormick, G.A., Wilde, D.K., and Wittmer, L.L. (1981). The 32b computer instruction decoding unit. *1981 IEEE International Solid-State Circuits Conference, XXIV*, 114–115 and 262. New York, USA. February 18–20.

Roesgen, J.P. (1986). The ADSP-2100 DSP microprocessor. *IEEE Micro*, 6(6), 49–59. December.

Ruckert, M. (2015). *The MMIX Supplement* – Supplement to The Art of Computer Programming Volumes 1, 2, 3 by Donald E. Knuth. Addison-Wesley.

Russell, C.T. (1992). In *The Galileo Mission*. Reprinted from Space Science Reviews. Russell, C.T. (ed.), 60(1–4). Kluwer Academic Publishers.

Russell, G. and Shaw, P. (1993). *Shifting Register Windows*. IEEE Micro, 13(4), 28–35. August.

Sailer, P.M. and Kaeli, D.R. (1996). *The DLX Instruction Set Architecture Handbook*. Morgan Kaufmann Publishers Inc.

Schmitt, O.H. (1938). A thermionic trigger. *Journal of Scientific Instruments*, 15(1), 24–26. January.

Shirriff, K. (2016). The surprising story of the first microprocessors. *IEEE Spectrum*, 53(9), 48–54. September.

Siewiorek, D.P., Bell, C.G., and Newell, A. (1982). *Computer Structures: Principles and Examples*. McGraw-Hill Computer Science Series. McGraw-Hill Book Company.

Silberman, J., Aoki, N., Boerstler, D., Burns, J.L., Dhong, S., Essbaum, A., Ghoshal, U., Heidel, D., Hofstee, P., Lee, K.T., Meltzer, D., Ngo, H., Nowka, K., Posluszny, S., Takahashi, O., Vo, I., and Zoric, B. (1998a). A 1.0 GHz single-issue 64 b PowerPC integer processor. *1998 IEEE International Solid-State Circuits Conference (ISSCC'98)*, 230–231. February 5–7.

Silberman, J., Aoki, N., Boerstler, D., Burns, J.L., Dhong, S., Essbaum, A., Ghoshal, U., Heidel, D., Hofstee, P., Lee, K.T., Meltzer, D., Ngo, H., Nowka, K., Posluszny, S., Takahashi, O., Vo, I., and Zoric, B. (1998b). A 1.0 GHz single-issue 64-bit powerPC integer processor. *IEEE Journal of Solid-State Circuits (JSSC)*, 33(11), 1600–1608. November.

Sites, R.L. (1979). How to use 1000 registers. *Caltech Conference on Very Large Scale Integration*, 527–532. California Institute of Technology, Pasadena, California (CA), USA. January 22–24.

Sites, R.L. (1993). Alpha AXP architecture. *Communications of the ACM (CACM)*, 36(2), 33–44. February.

Smith, J.E. (1989). Dynamic instruction scheduling and the astronautics ZS-I. *IEEE Computer*, 22(7), 21–35. July.

Stachniak, Z. (2010). The MIL MF7114 microprocessor. *IEEE Annals of the History of Computing*, 32(4), 48–58. October/December.

Stallings, W. (1986). In *Reduced Instruction Set Computers – Tutorial*. Stallings, W. (ed.). IEEE Computer Society Press.

Stevens, W.Y. (1964). The structure of SYSTEM/360. Part II: System implementations. *IBM Systems Journal*, 3(2), 136–143.

Stewart, L.C., Payne, A.C., and Levergood, T.M. (1992). Are DSP chips obsolete? Technical report CRL 92/10. Cambridge Research Lab. Digital Equipment Corporation. November 16.

Sun (1987). The SPARC Architecture Manual. Sun Microsystems Inc.

Sutherland, I.E. (1989). Micropipelines. *Communications of the ACM (CACM)*, 32(6), 720–738. June.

Sutherland, I. and Ebergen, J. (2002). Ordinateurs asynchrones. *Pour la Science*, no. 301. November.

Suzuoki, M., Kutaragi, K., Hiroi, T., Magoshi, H., Okamoto, S., Oka, M., Ohba, A., Yamamoto, Y., Furuhashi, M., Tanaka, M., Yutaka, T., Okada, T., Nagamatsu, M., Urakawa, Y., Funyu, M., Kunimatsu, A., Goto, H., Hashimoto, K., Ide, N, Murakami, H., Ohtaguro, Y., and Aono, A. (1999). A microprocessor with a 128-Bit CPU, ten floating-point MAC's, four floating-point dividers, and an MPEG-2 decoder. *IEEE Journal of Solid-State Circuits (JSSC)*, 34(11), 1608–1618. November.

Thomas, A.T. (1976). Architecture and applications of a 12-bit CMOS microprocessor. *Proceedings of the IEEE*, 64(6), 873–881. June.

TI (1976). TMS 9900 Microprocessor Data Manual. Texas Instruments Incorporated. December.

TI (1997). CMOS power consumption and C_{pd} calculation. Application Note SCAA035B. Texas Instruments. June.

Titus, J. (1974). Computer! build the mark 8 minicomputer. *Radio-Electronics*, 45(7), 29–33. July.

Tomasulo, R.M. (1967). An efficient algorithm for exploiting multiple arithmetic units. *IBM Journal of Research and Development*, 11(1), 25–33. January.

Travers, M. (2015). CPU power consumption experiments and results analysis of Intel i7-4820K. Technical report NCL-EEEMICRO-TR-2015-197. School of Electrical and Electronic Engineering, Newcastle University.

Tredennick, N. (1996). Microprocessor-based computers. *IEEE Computer*, 29(10), 27–37. October.

Tullsen, D.M., Eggers. S.J., and Levy, H.M. (1995). Simultaneous multithreading: Maximizing on-chip parallelism. *22nd Annual International Symposium on Computer Architecture (ISCA)*, 392–403. Santa Margherita Ligure, Italy. June 22–24.

Tullsen, D.M., Eggers, S.J., Emery, J.S., Levy, H.M., Lo, J.L., and Stammy, R.L. (1996). Exploiting choice: Instruction fetch and issue on an implementable simultaneous multithreading processor. *23nd Annual International Symposium on Computer Architecture (ISCA)*, 191–202. Philadelphia, Pennsylvania, USA. May 22–24.

Ungerer, T., Robic, B., and Šilc, J. (2003). A survey of processors with explicit multithreading. *ACM Computing Surveys (CSUR) Surveys*, 35(1), 29–63. March.

Vajda, F. (1986). Super micros – objectives and approaches. *Microprocessing and Microprogramming*, 17(1), 1–17. January.

van de Goor, A.J. (1989). *Computer Architecture and Design*. Addison-Wesley Publishing Company, Inc.

Wagner, K.D. (1988). Clock system design. *IEEE Design & Test of Computers*, 5(5), 9–27. October.

Weaver, D.L. and Germond, T. (1994, 2000). In *The SPARC Architecture Manual, Version 9*. Weaver, D.L. and Germond, T. (eds). SPARC International, Inc., Prentice Hall.

Weissberger, A.J. (1975). Keeping pace with a single-chip 16-bit microprocessor. *1975 National Computer Conference and Exposition (AFIPS'75)*, 9–14. Anaheim, California, USA. May 19–22.

Whitworth, I. (1979). Review of microprocessor architecture. *Microprocessors and Microsystems*, 3(1), 21–28. January–February.

Whitworth, I. (1980). Developments in 16-bit microprocessors. *Microprocessors and Microsystems*, 4(1), 17–22. January–February.

Winder, R.O. (1974). WPM 6.6: COSMAC – A COS/MOS. SESSION VI: LSI logic. *1974 IEEE International Solid-State Circuits Conference (ISSCC 74)*, XVII, 64–65. Philadelphia, PA, USA. February 13–15.

Witten, I.H. and Cleary, J.G. (1983). An introduction to the architecture of the Intel iAPX 432. *Software & Microsystems*, 2(2), 29–34. April.

Young, L., Bennett, T., and Lavell, J. (1974). N-channel MOS technology yields new generation of microprocessors. Technical articles. *Electronics*, 47(8), 88–95. April 18.

Young, I.A., Greason, J.K., and Wong, K.L. (1992). A PLL clock generator with 5 to 110 MHz of lock range for microprocessors. *IEEE Journal of Solid-State Circuits (JSSC)*, 27(11), 1599–1607. November.

Index

This index covers all 5 volumes in this series of books.

digital, § V4-1.2.4.5.1, V4-1.2.4.5.2,
V4-2.8.4.2 *and* V4-3.4.2
firmware, § V1-1.4, V2-3.1, V4-5.7 *and*
V5-3.5
BIOS, § V4-5.9 *and* V5-3.5.3
EFI, § V5-3.5.3
microcode, § V4-2.5.7
monitor, § V4-V4-5.7, V5-2.1.1, V5-
2.2.4, V5-2.2.5, V5-2.2.7, V5-3.1,
V5-3.2.1 *and* V5-3.5.1
open firmware, § V5-3.5.4
POST, § V5-2.2.1, V5-3.2.1, V5-3.2.2,
V5-3.5.3 *and* V5-3.5.4
UEFI, § V5-3.5.3
flag, *cf. code/condition*
flip-flop, § V1-1.2, V1-2.3, V1-3.1.4, V1-
3.3.1.2.1, V1-3.3.1.2.2, V2-1.3, V2-3.1,
V3-2.4.1, V3-3.1.1, V4-5.2.3, V4-5.3
and V5-2.2.5
flow, § V1-3.1.2 *and* V1-3.1.3, V2-1.5,
V3-3.1.5.1 *and* V4-5.2
control, § V1-3.1.2
exceptional (ECF), § V1-3.1.2
graph (CFG), § V1-3.1.2
data flow, § V1-3.1.2
form factor, § V1-1.2, V5-3.4.1 *and* V5-
3.4.2
AT, ATX, BTX, ITX, NLX, PC, WTX
and XT, V5-3.4.1
format
binary, *cf. binary format*
file, *cf. file format*
instruction, *cf. instruction format*
Fourier transform, § V3-5.2
discrete, § V4-1.2.4.5.2
fast, *cf.* § V3-5.2, V4-1.2.4.5.2 *and* V4-
3.4.4
FPGA, § V1-3.5.3, V2-4.2.10, V4-5.7
and V5-2.2.3
frame, *cf. memory*
FSM, *cf. state/state machine*
function, *cf. subprogram*

G

gate, *cf. transistor/gate*
glue logic, § V3-2.1.1.1, V3-2.3, V5-3.1
to V5-3.3 *and* V5-3.4.2
grid
crossbar matrix, § V2-3.3.6, V2-4.2.7
and V2-4.2.9
electronic tube, § V1-1.2
GSI, *cf. integration technology*

H

HAL (Hardware Abstraction Layer), §
V5-1.1.4
hardware development tool
development system, § V5-2.2.3 *and*
V5-2.2.7
emulator, § V5-2.2.3
hardware, § V5-2.2.3, V5-2.2.4.3
and V5-2.2.6
ICE, § V5-2.2.3 *and* V5-2.2.7
programmer, § V5-2.1.2
hardware interface
microprocessor, § V3-2.2
RS-232, § V2-1.3, V3-5.3, V5-2.1.1,
V5-2.1.2, V5-2.2.1 *and* V5-2.2.4.1
SCSI, § V2-1.2, V2-2.2.3, V2-4.2.6,
V2-4.3 *and* V5-3.3.1
HMT (Hardware MultiThreading), § V1-
3.4.3.2 *and* V3-4.7
hot plugging, § V2-3.1 *and* V5-1.1.4
HPC (High-Performance Computing), §
V1-1.2

I

I/O
isolated (IIO) or separated, §
V3-2.1.1.1

Other titles from

in

Computer Engineering

2020

LAFFLY Dominique
*TORUS 1 – Toward an Open Resource Using Services: Cloud Computing
for Environmental Data*
*TORUS 2 – Toward an Open Resource Using Services: Cloud Computing
for Environmental Data*
*TORUS 3 – Toward an Open Resource Using Services: Cloud Computing
for Environmental Data*

LAURENT Anne, LAURENT Dominique, MADERA Cédrine
Data Lakes
(Databases and Big Data Set – Volume 2)

OULHADJ Hamouche, DAACHI Boubaker, MENASRI Riad
Metaheuristics for Robotics
(Optimization Heuristics Set – Volume 2)

SADIQUI Ali
Computer Network Security

DEROUSSI Laurent
Metaheuristics for Logistics
(Metaheuristics Set – Volume 4)

DHAENENS Clarisse and JOURDAN Laetitia
Metaheuristics for Big Data
(Metaheuristics Set – Volume 5)

LABADIE Nacima, PRINS Christian, PRODHON Caroline
Metaheuristics for Vehicle Routing Problems
(Metaheuristics Set – Volume 3)

LEROY Laure
Eyestrain Reduction in Stereoscopy

LUTTON Evelyne, PERROT Nathalie, TONDA Albert
Evolutionary Algorithms for Food Science and Technology
(Metaheuristics Set – Volume 7)

MAGOULÈS Frédéric, ZHAO Hai-Xiang
Data Mining and Machine Learning in Building Energy Analysis

RIGO Michel
Advanced Graph Theory and Combinatorics

2015

BARBIER Franck, RECOUSSINE Jean-Luc
COBOL Software Modernization: From Principles to Implementation with the BLU AGE® Method

CHEN Ken
Performance Evaluation by Simulation and Analysis with Applications to Computer Networks

CLERC Maurice
Guided Randomness in Optimization
(Metaheuristics Set – Volume 1)

DURAND Nicolas, GIANAZZA David, GOTTELAND Jean-Baptiste, ALLIOT Jean-Marc
Metaheuristics for Air Traffic Management
(Metaheuristics Set – Volume 2)

MAGOULÈS Frédéric, ROUX François-Xavier, HOUZEAUX Guillaume
Parallel Scientific Computing

MUNEESAWANG Paisarn, YAMMEN Suchart
Visual Inspection Technology in the Hard Disk Drive Industry

2014

BOULANGER Jean-Louis
Formal Methods Applied to Industrial Complex Systems

BOULANGER Jean-Louis
Formal Methods Applied to Complex Systems:Implementation of the B Method

GARDI Frédéric, BENOIST Thierry, DARLAY Julien, ESTELLON Bertrand, MEGEL Romain
Mathematical Programming Solver based on Local Search

KRICHEN Saoussen, CHAOUACHI Jouhaina
Graph-related Optimization and Decision Support Systems

LARRIEU Nicolas, VARET Antoine
Rapid Prototyping of Software for Avionics Systems: Model-oriented Approaches for Complex Systems Certification

OUSSALAH Mourad Chabane
Software Architecture 1
Software Architecture 2

PASCHOS Vangelis Th
Combinatorial Optimization – 3-volume series, 2nd Edition
Concepts of Combinatorial Optimization – Volume 1, 2nd Edition
Problems and New Approaches – Volume 2, 2nd Edition
Applications of Combinatorial Optimization – Volume 3, 2nd Edition

QUESNEL Flavien
Scheduling of Large-scale Virtualized Infrastructures: Toward Cooperative Management

RIGO Michel
Formal Languages, Automata and Numeration Systems 1:
Introduction to Combinatorics on Words
Formal Languages, Automata and Numeration Systems 2:
Applications to Recognizability and Decidability

SAINT-DIZIER Patrick
Musical Rhetoric: Foundations and Annotation Schemes

TOUATI Sid, DE DINECHIN Benoit
Advanced Backend Optimization

2013

ANDRÉ Etienne, SOULAT Romain
The Inverse Method: Parametric Verification of Real-time Embedded Systems

BOULANGER Jean-Louis
Safety Management for Software-based Equipment

DELAHAYE Daniel, PUECHMOREL Stéphane
Modeling and Optimization of Air Traffic

FRANCOPOULO Gil
LMF — Lexical Markup Framework

GHÉDIRA Khaled
Constraint Satisfaction Problems

ROCHANGE Christine, UHRIG Sascha, SAINRAT Pascal
Time-Predictable Architectures

WAHBI Mohamed
Algorithms and Ordering Heuristics for Distributed Constraint Satisfaction Problems

2009

FOURNIER Jean-Claude
Graph Theory and Applications

GUEDON Jeanpierre
The Mojette Transform / Theory and Applications

JARD Claude, ROUX Olivier
Communicating Embedded Systems / Software and Design

LECOUTRE Christophe
Constraint Networks / Targeting Simplicity for Techniques and Algorithms

2008

BANÂTRE Michel, MARRÓN Pedro José, OLLERO Hannibal, WOLITZ Adam
Cooperating Embedded Systems and Wireless Sensor Networks

MERZ Stephan, NAVET Nicolas
Modeling and Verification of Real-time Systems

PASCHOS Vangelis Th
Combinatorial Optimization and Theoretical Computer Science: Interfaces and Perspectives

WALDNER Jean-Baptiste
Nanocomputers and Swarm Intelligence

2007

BENHAMOU Frédéric, JUSSIEN Narendra, O'SULLIVAN Barry
Trends in Constraint Programming

JUSSIEN Narendra
A TO Z OF SUDOKU

2006

BABAU Jean-Philippe *et al.*
From MDD Concepts to Experiments and Illustrations – DRES 2006

HABRIAS Henri, FRAPPIER Marc
Software Specification Methods

MURAT Cecile, PASCHOS Vangelis Th
Probabilistic Combinatorial Optimization on Graphs

PANETTO Hervé, BOUDJLIDA Nacer
*Interoperability for Enterprise Software and Applications 2006 / IFAC-IFIP
I-ESA'2006*

2005

GÉRARD Sébastien *et al.*
Model Driven Engineering for Distributed Real Time Embedded Systems

PANETTO Hervé
Interoperability of Enterprise Software and Applications 2005

Printed and bound by CPI Group (UK) Ltd, Croydon, CR0 4YY

27/10/2024

14580734-0003